Harry Boyle

HARRY BOYLE was born on a farm near Goderich, Ontario, and is widely known for his witty and nostalgic newspaper articles, some of the best of which have been collected for this book. At one time or another the author has been a hobo, a creator of outstanding radio programs for the C.B.C., and a playwright. He is Vice Chairman of the Canadian Radio-Television Commission. Another collection of his boyhood reminiscences appeared in the book *Homebrew and Patches* – which is also available in PaperJacks. This is what the Toronto *Globe and Mail* says about Harry Boyle's writing in these books: "Once in a long, long time the reviewer, to his utter surprise, reads a book that has everything the publishers claim for it . . . There ought to be some sort of prize for it . . . Everything is told in a simple, heartwarming style, with a complete absence of sophistication and a real grassroots affection for what he remembers. It is the warmth, honesty, and simplicity that lift these books high above the commonplace."

MOSTLY IN CLOVER

HARRY J. BOYLE

with a foreword by
BURTON T. RICHARDSON

PaperJacks

A division of General Publishing Co. Limited
Don Mills, Ontario

Originally published 1963
by Clarke, Irwin & Co. Ltd.
Published in PaperJacks 1972

ISBN 0-7737-7007-0

Printed and bound in Canada

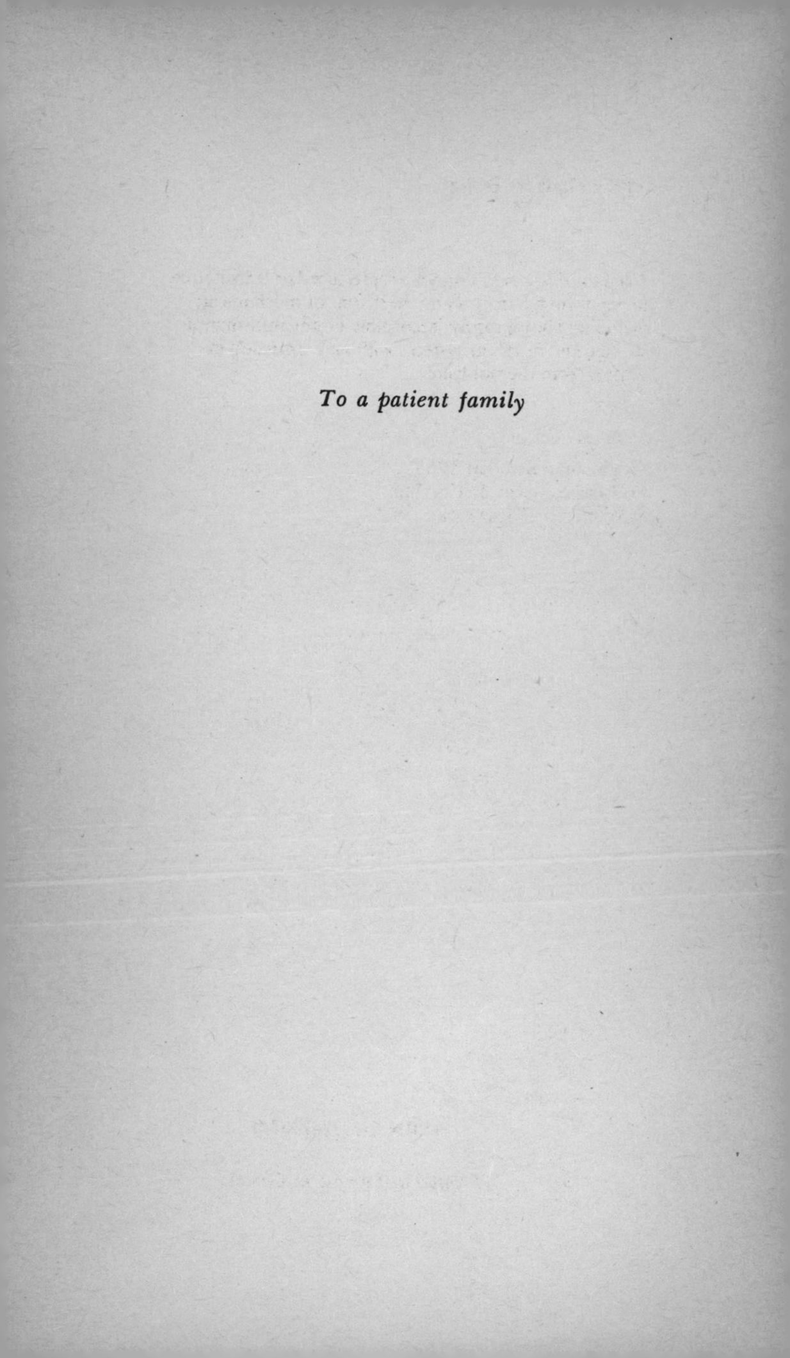

To a patient family

CONTENTS

FOREWORD

Some of Harry Boyle's articles may be found, in yellowed newsprint clippings, pinned to kitchen walls in rural Ontario. Others are carried in wallets of city folk, as memory warmers of forgotten days on the farm. For five years, Mr. Boyle has been a contributor to *The Telegram*, and *Mostly In Clover* is a selection of his articles, edited for book publication and rescued for a wider immortality than comes to most material published in a daily newspaper.

If there is any doubt of the geographical location of the farm and the small town of which Harry Boyle writes, it is dispelled by the fact that he was born forty-six years ago on a farm in Huron County, near Goderich. The life of that farm, of the cross-roads store which his uncle operated, and of the schools he attended has vanished into Ontario's past. But it exists in the magic of Harry Boyle's memory, which is an open door to an era full of warm nostalgia. A marvellous power to evoke the sounds and sights and smells and feelings of a boyhood gone these four decades commands the eye and the heart of the reader in every page of Boyle's writing.

Some of his most memorable passages refer to food. Harry Boyle has a truly mouth-watering style, as in his report, forty years after, of a Sunday dinner on the farm:

> Those chickens were a delight to look at. They were shaded from light golden on the breast where they had been covered with some strips of salt pork, to a deep brown on the drumsticks. When the thread over the cavity was slit there wafted up an aroma of onion and sage from the dressing. As I sat there, it was almost impossible to control the digestive juices in my mouth.

Then the steaming gravy-boat, the mashed turnips, the bowl of green beans, the corn on the cob "stacked on great plates like poles waiting for a 'wood buzzing'." And the dessert? "Apple pie with a flaky crust, the apples immersed in a caramel-like syrup accompanied by cheese that nipped your tongue vied for attention with pumpkin pie covered with great gobs of whipped cream."

Harry Boyle chronicles his boyhood as a lyric remembrance. After Sunday dinner, the children found a spot in the shade outside and talked "about the mysteries of the world outside the valley, which were beginning to intrigue them."

In that world beyond the valley of childhood, Harry Boyle became a broadcaster and a writer. Readers have written to *The Telegram* to describe Harry Boyle's writing with warm affection. One called it "priceless." Another wrote: "I find his column one of the most refreshing bits of country air I've whiffed in a long time. Living the hectic life of an urban citizen, it's nice to reflect once in a while on a life I'd almost forgotten." Another asked: "Who is Harry J. Boyle?"

The answer to that question is that Harry Boyle is radio programme development officer for the Canadian Broadcasting Corporation in Toronto. One chapter in his life justifies the label given him by a magazine writer of "an ex-hobo." A dozen years ago, when the controversy over the place of culture in broadcasting was in its infancy, Harry Boyle was the creative force behind the "CBC Wednesday Night" series on the Trans-Canada Network. He still is "the rumpled man with the farmer's face," and "a hulking, red-faced, blondish product of rural Ontario who still looks as though he had slept in his clothes."

He is more than that. He is a creative broadcaster, an eloquent conversationalist, a playwright, and a fine and meticulous author of the best short articles about a homespun boyhood in rural Ontario that have ever appeared in a daily newspaper.

Burton T. Richardson
1961

WINTER

1

THE WINTER BATTLE

THEY SAY WE LIVE IN A STATE OF COLD WAR. In the country, only a matter of a few years ago, we lived for an excessive number of months in a state of constant war against the cold. From early November until mid-April the battle of preparedness and emergency measures was the normal state for a countryman.

During those days the sight of a stranger getting off the train and walking into the village gave a good idea of what it meant to have a lack of adequate armament. His teeth would be chattering while he tried to keep his overcoat down. In plain words, he didn't have on winter underwear. Modern comics who make fun of "long Johns" should have had an exposure to our winter weather. It would have taken a lot of the humour out of the situation.

There's more to this matter of long underwear than you might suspect. For years there has been a division of opinion over the matter of fleece-lined and all-wool. Father was a fleece-line follower but Grandfather maintained that only sissies would wear fleece-lined.

"Those fleece ones get damp and they stay damp. Take pure wool now, it absorbs the dampness and then your body heat will sort of evaporate it."

This was the reason for Grandfather's waiting every year until the 24th of May before he took off his second, or outer, suit of woollen underwear. The inner, or permanent, suit he maintained during the entire summer on the theory that it helped to soak up the sweat. He may have been right at that. On the hottest day in the hay or the harvest field he never seemed to be affected by the heat.

There was also an argument about the merits of shirt and drawers as opposed to combinations. The older men stuck with the shirt and drawers but younger men seemed to have a liking for the one-piecers. The women were inclined, if they were the frugal type, to suggest that their husbands take the two-piecers. When a pair of drawers wore out they were simpler and cheaper to replace than a pair of combinations. Driving down the concession on a frosty day, especially if it was a Monday, you could tell at a glance from the skeletons dancing on the clotheslines who were combination men.

In Murphy's store there was a small counter at the back where the smocks, overalls and underwear were piled up. The women would flap the underwear around and argue about the merits of fleece-lined and woollen, as if *they* were going to wear it, not their husbands. Then there was the matter of weight. The woollen underwear came in different weights and was priced accordingly.

There was a never-ending argument about the merits of the two leading brands of underwear—Stanfield's and Penman's. Murphy would be called in to arbitrate. He had a very red nose, and a paunch covered by a one-time white apron, and he wore a flat straw hat in the store, summer and winter. A stub of a pencil was stuck behind his right ear and he was forever looking for it when he went to make up an account.

"Now, Mr. Murphy, you must know which of these two would be the best. I declare they're getting so expensive that a body has to get the best value."

Murphy would clear his throat and look helplessly to the front of the store where the men would be pretending not to listen.

"Well, they're both good. No complaints at all. Some may take a fancy to one but, on the other hand, others swear by the other."

He delivered this triumphantly in the vain hope that he had settled the matter.

"Do you really think the heavy one is worth the money, Mr. Murphy?"

"Depends on the man. Big man needs the heavy, I think."

That finished the discussion.

We once had a hired man who seemed attached to his underwear. My mother nudged my father one day just before Christmas and said, "I don't think that man has changed his underwear since he came here last fall."

Father, engrossed in the newspaper, grunted, "Maybe he doesn't wear any underwear."

Mother pondered on this. The man had been hired to help clear a slash of woods and he was boarding in, and sleeping in the room over the kitchen.

"He does so wear underwear. I've seen it when he had his shirt sleeves rolled up, and it looks filthy."

Father wasn't much help.

"Maybe he washes it himself."

"Now you tell him that I'll wash it for him. Goodness, he may have crawly things on him."

"I'm not going to tell any man to take his underwear off. He may only have one suit."

That state existed all winter. Mother hinted to the man and he blandly paid no attention to her. She threatened Father with everything and Father paid no attention to her. She resorted to Grandfather, who paid no attention to her.

One Saturday night, as spring was coming, the hired man came out of the store with a parcel under his arm. Next morning, when Father came down to light the fire in the kitchen stove, he found the remains of the winter underwear still glowing. Some time in the night it had been offered up as a fiery sacrifice to spring.

Billy Joe Hawkins got the name of "Itchy" because of underwear. He married a girl from the city who made the mistake of asking her bridesmaid, a local girl with a yen for

Billy Joe, if there was anything she should know. The girl told her to be sure to starch his underwear.

Indoor stoves were our main line of defence against the cold. Now, every time the furnace gives a throaty rumble and then purrs on as it gives out heat, I am thankful. This sense of gratitude comes from the fact that we now are relatively free of those task-masters known as stoves.

However, it is pleasant to think about the old parlour stove. On Sunday evenings it would blaze away cheerfully, the flames winking at us through the broken mica in the front door. It looked bulky and substantial and we knew that for one night, at least, the bedroom floors above the parlour wouldn't be ice cold on our bare feet.

Sunday evening was a pleasant one. There would be a plate of Spy apples from the bins in the cellar and a few sips of cider when Mother wasn't looking. This was also the evening for playing the old wind-up phonograph with the wax cylinders. The machine, guarded during the week, was reserved solely for Sunday evening entertainment. Crackling noisily, the old stove sat through those comfortable hours. It had a fat base for the ash pan, surrounded by nickel bars. Then it tapered up to the fire-box with the mica-windowed door. Over all there was a sort of nickelled tiara that could be swung aside if we wanted to put a kettle on the one lid to heat.

As a boy I was very fond of that stove. It had character and a certain dignity. By the time I had grown up, I hated it, right from the three-foot-square, gaudily decorated, tin-covered board it stood on, to its nickelled tiara. My hatred was confined to spring and autumn when it had to be moved.

There was an unwritten law in our household that this Buddha-like creation had to be taken out to the back woodshed for the summer months and then returned in the autumn when the weather started to get nippy.

When the first sign of frost appeared in the fall there would be a gentle hint from Mother about bringing the stove into the parlour. A man, of course, is never expected to respond to the first hint about such a domestic problem.

Next, there was considerable talk about the way the weather was turning cold. Weather forecasts would be mentioned. The almanac would invariably support the contention that there might even be snow in October.

Finally there would come a day when all the stove-pipes were laid out freshly varnished on the back stoop. Father did not appear to notice them; it's amazing how little a man can notice when he wants to.

"Did you see those stove-pipes out there?"

"What stove-pipes?"

"Don't be silly. That stove goes up before you go back to the barn."

"But I have to go over to help Ed this afternoon."

"Ed can wait."

Ed would wait as Father and the hired man, or one of us boys, walked to the woodshed and looked at the iron monster. It was strange how friendly and warm that stove looked in the winter and how ugly and forbidding at this time.

There it sat, looking like one of those squat, heavy-set Japanese wrestlers, and we could just imagine it saying, "Come on, just try and take me."

The amazing thing was that that stove seemed to have nothing but sharp edges. When we picked it up, the legs fell off, and if one of us slipped and dropped it, it would come down most solidly on his foot. The thing seemed to weigh a ton, and going up the steps from the woodshed into the kitchen we would be slammed by the tiara we had forgotten to take off the lid, or just plain pushed in the face by the door that ordinarily opened only with effort, but now came open easily by itself.

This stove would go through the door, but only by way of a desperate sort of manipulation. We jiggled and joggled and then tried by brute force to push it through. The lady of the house would immediately scream that we were scraping the fresh paint off the door jamb. Then it would be decided that we should take the door off its hinges.

The fact of the matter is that we had never been able to get the stove through without taking the door from its hinges. We had also never been able to resist trying.

Having negotiated the doorway into the kitchen, there was still the matter of getting it through without putting it down. The sharp edges were simply murder on the linoleum and would cut a neat pattern every time. Thus, there would be a furious sort of dog-trot across the kitchen, made necessary by the sheer torture resulting from the lurching of the monster from side to side, while Mother yelled navigational instructions as we managed to bump from the kitchen stove to the table to the sideboard to the parlour door.

Fortunately, the latter was wide, so there was no difficulty in this quarter. The trouble came in the parlour. Another thick layer of varnish had been added, a tradition each spring, so that no one quite agreed on where the stove used to sit. After more bloody fingers and argument the board was placed and the monster was put down on it.

This was never the end of our tribulations, however. There was the matter of putting legs on the thing. Prop up one side and hook them in and then lift the other side and the ones attached spread out. We lifted the stove while Mother tried to put them in. When we yelled from the pain of it she got mad and started to cry and all the time the monster grinned on.

Then we started to match stove-pipes. I'll spare you that. The devil invented stove-pipes just to try man's patience. When the stove was all set up the hired man threatened to quit, and Mother wouldn't speak to Father, who had to wear mitts for three days because the palms of his hands were so sore.

Just the same, on that first really chilly Sunday evening when the fire was going, the varnish burning from the pipes, and the flames were winking at us through the mica, we could even begin to like the monster again.

There was a great deal of comfort to be derived from the old stoves. No furnace could give the solid warmth that came from sitting around the range on a cold winter evening when the wind was snickering at the eaves and rattling the windows. The height of bliss was to roast stockinged feet on the oven door while the cat slept contentedly on a rug and the tea-kettle burbled and hissed with promise of a good cup of tea.

The old heater in the front room was the centre of attraction on a Sunday evening when the flames glowed and flickered behind the mica windows in its front. When the beech and maple blocks burned down to a mass of glowing coals it was time to toast some apples on the end of sticks or brown a piece of home-made bread and then douse it liberally with sweet churned butter. Every time I go in the front room now, I miss that stove.

The thought of stoves always makes me feel a great deal of sympathy for my father. It was a feeling I didn't have as a boy. Experience, however, has taught me that he had a definite grievance when he complained that no matter how he tried he was always called upon to light the first fires in the two stoves that kept our house on the farm in a warm condition.

On some mornings, from his bed, he would announce in a voice that could be heard a mile away, that he wasn't feeling very well. This announcement came about a quarter to five in the morning. It would be a dark and very cold winter morning. Shortly afterwards there would be a loud and prolonged series of groans, designed to move the stoniest boyish heart to some form of sympathetic consideration. However, his pitiful groans would be followed by dead silence, except for the moaning of the frost-soaked house or the scraping of a tree branch on the outside wall. We all knew that if there really had been anything wrong with him, Mother would have been up and had us downstairs in a jiffy.

Finally, exasperated by the lack of response, Father would say in his loud voice, "I could die in this icebox and not a soul would even help me by lighting the fire."

Still there would be no response, as my brother and I huddled in the protective warmth of the feather bed. We were playing possum, and then Mother would say in her best martyr's voice, "Oh, I'll get up and light the fire." This was the signal for the "dance of the bare feet." Father would hop out of bed and then frantically dance around the frosty, cold floor, searing the soles of his feet as he tried to get into his pants with the braces getting snarled up, or else he would plunge a foot in, only to find the leg turned in, the way he had left it the night before.

There were times when Father would roar and give me a direct order to go and light the fires. When he used that tone of voice, he meant business. It was torture trying to dress under the covers and I usually went hippety-hopping down the stairs with one leg in the overalls and one out, and the shirt-tail flying. It was a race to the kitchen, in the hope that there might be some coals left in the kitchen range. A dry block on a bed of coals was a cinch to start. No such luck!

Then there would come the painful memory that I had been told to put kindling in the oven to dry. Father had noticed the omission and that's why he had commanded me to light the fire. The woodshed was colder even than outside and there would be a drift of snow from a crack in the wall, neatly covering the kindling. The kindling wouldn't burn.

On one occasion when the fire was particularly stubborn, I tried some dry straw. When Father came down and paused to inspect the fire he was greeted with a blast of fluffy ash in his face.

Mother was death on the use of coal oil. This was a ruse we often tried as a short cut, but Mother was always afraid that it might explode. If either my brother or I had been shanghaied into lighting the fire we had to run the gauntlet of Mother's inquiry. She would come into the kitchen and start sniffing suspiciously. If there was the least taint of coal oil, real or imaginary, we would get pulled by the ear and told, "If I catch either of you using coal oil on that fire, I'll tan you good."

I feel somewhat ashamed now of the tricks we played to get out of the fire-lighting ceremony. We always managed to get ashes on the floor, chips on the parlour rug, or to bump into the stove-pipes and set them just enough askew that they smoked. Mother would say, "Those boys can't light a fire. If you don't want to do it, I'll do it myself." This always defeated Father.

But he had his own form of revenge.

The parlour was directly below our bedroom. Father, after being forced back to stove duty, would keep up an unceasing din as he worked. Shortly after the kindling started to crackle and stove-pipes "pinged" with heat, he would shake down the parlour stove. He shook it in earnest. It was the noisiest shaking-down you could imagine. Everything clanked and banged. The door would slam shut. Then the ornamental top was swung out and the lid was given a few taps. The doors would come open and shut again.

That was only the start of the campaign. The pipes would be tapped to knock the soot down. The damper would scrape and squeal and growl as it was adjusted and then readjusted. The ash bucket would be "whanged" a few times. Then there would be a brief silence, followed shortly by a great thumping, as an armful of wood was dropped in the ornamental woodbox. As if that weren't enough, Father would start in his fog-horn baritone to massacre a hymn or a cowboy ballad.

We would try and stuff our ears but the voice would come rolling up the stairway, asking sarcastically, "Would your royal selves come down and get warm? COME DOWN NOW!"

By this time, however, the pipes would be ticking with heat and we could huddle and dress in relative comfort. By the time the chores were finished Father would be in better humour and we would go off to school to roast on one side and freeze on the other beside the old box stove.

Just the same, nowadays when I hear the furnace come on I feel a little guilty about the stove feud that we waged with Father on those cold winter mornings so many years ago.

2
COLD DAYS

WHEN WE WENT TO BED IT WAS COLD, with gusty winds that seemed to scatter the clouds around in magnificent disarray. There were pinpricks of stars against the gray sea of sky. Earlier in the day there had been a swirling series of dry, sandy, snow-flurries but they didn't amount to much.

Grandfather had been listening to the wind, a cold pipe held absently in his hand. We noticed him rubbing his stockinged feet together a few times, but thought it was only the chilblains. Then he got up and opened the kitchen door and we could hear the banshee wail of the express in the far valley. It was a sound we seldom heard, except, as he said, when there was a change due in the weather.

"We're due for a change to-night," he finally pronounced.

"Softer?"

"Aye, it will be softer. Could be rain or snow."

Having made his statement he picked up the little coal-oil lamp and with a muttered farewell went to his room.

"Can't see how it can change that quickly," said Mother taking off her glasses and putting the mending away.

"He's usually right," yawned Father, who, spotting us, suddenly ordered, "You two! Off to bed."

Through the chilly hall and up past the lamp that was turned low at the landing, shucking clothes on the way and then plunging under the covers and kneeling to say hasty prayers under the protective canopy of the quilts—this was a nightly ritual. Then, with only foreheads and noses exposed, we listened for a time to the wind gusts before we went to sleep. At some point I can remember waking up and hearing the snatching, green fingers of the pines scraping on the frosted window of the bedroom. Later on in the night I can dimly remember sensing a sort of calm. It seemed as if the world had come to a standstill and even the old house didn't creak anymore. I could have gone and scratched at the frost on the window to see the change myself, but it was too comfortable in that warm bed.

In the morning a magical transformation had come about. The ugly, fall-scarred world lay under a carpet of magic, white down. Some time during the night, as Grandpa had predicted, the weather had "softened," and the great, bulky, soft flakes of snow had come tumbling down from the heavens. It was still coming down. When we looked out we couldn't even see the barn, and the snow lay in great drifts everywhere.

There is something fascinating about the transformation that a real snowstorm can bring to the world. After the autumn agony of losing their leaves, the naked trees are given the consolation of narrow, white strips along the trunks and branches, and even the twigs are given a dab of the stuff. The snow is bulked over the edge of the eaves and sits like comical caps on the fence posts. It even gives a rakish look to the old wooden pump with its dangling arm.

The forgotten democrat behind the driving-shed has a load of fresh snow. The stupid old hen that has eluded us for days, finds herself trying to wade out of the orchard from her hiding place, in an attempt to get to the safety of the hen-house.

Grandpa said on this occasion, with a wrinkle of his whiskers, "Those corns of mine haven't failed me in thirty, going on thirty-five years, when it comes to predicting a soft spell. Aye, and when you hear the express from that far away, it's a sign."

My brother and I weren't thinking of omens, though. Can there be greater fun for a boy than to make tracks in fresh snow? Stamp around the ring and lay out the design for the fox and goose; see if it is wet enough to be rolled into a snowman; pelt Father with a snowball when he is carrying the milk pails. This is one time when you can get away with it. There's a strange lightheartedness when the world turns shiny-white, and clean after a snowstorm like this one.

We went to school, and even the teacher was in good humour. The air was soft and the snow still coming down slowly. Almost imperceptibly it was getting colder. We didn't notice it right away because our scarves, gloves and stocking caps, as well as our coats, were ranged with those of all the others in a steaming ring around the old box stove, and the school had the humid and woolly smell of sheep-shearing time.

Before the last recess the sky had darkened.

The teacher was city born, and didn't understand country storms. We could hear the knife-edge of the wind as the softness changed to cold. It made us a little afraid, but when one of the older boys suggested that we go home the teacher looked surprised and told him to sit down. She wasn't falling for a story like that. It was a wonderful day as far as she was concerned.

Just before last recess one of the trustees came and called for his two daughters and warned her that it was starting to blow. After that she looked frightened and dismissed us. It was none too soon, because by the time we got down the concession to our place the drifts were packing across the road like rows of hard razors. The wind blew icy pellets of snow, and when we turned in the laneway it swooped up from the hollow and practically held us at a standstill.

This was a day for doing the chores early. It was a fight to get from the barn to the house and we had to bring in extra wood from the woodshed for the old heater in the front room. All the stoves were stoked up, and although the old house creaked like a ghostly galleon on high seas, there was a great air of comfort inside.

It was a night when the family felt close together. By common accord we moved into the front room and somebody brought up a bowl of Spy apples from the cellar. Grandpa had a story to tell of the time he worked in the lumber camps, and Father told of when he had been a deckhand on a lake freighter during a November storm. Father didn't make us go to bed as early as usual because it was a foregone conclusion that there wouldn't be school the next day.

The storm roared on all the next day. Chores were the only essential work. The rest of the time we could read and lazy away inside the snug fortifications of the house. It was a comfortable and satisfying feeling. We listened for the battle reports over the party telephone. The mailman had to turn back. Three teams broke the sideroad as far as the tenth concession, to get Con Mackay to the doctor. Everybody in the township had a worrying feeling about Mrs. Tim McGrath because it was known that her baby was due at any time.

The fires were stoked and we had time for another trip through the collection of stereopticon slides. Listening to the roar of the ocean in the conch shell that Aunt Meg had brought back from Atlantic City, we heard Mother telling with a sort of sweet sadness of the honeymoon trip she and Father had made to Niagara Falls.

The normal and petty bickering of a family was forgotten. Grandpa snoozed and smoked and talked. Father read most of the time. Mother was busy baking bread because of the fear of how long the storm would last, so the house had a friendly, yeasty smell.

After two days the storm broke and the men of the township put snow plows on their sleighs and cleared the road. The mail came through and we had to go back to school, following the sharp furrows of the newly opened road, with a sort of bitter-sweet feeling of loneliness because the storm had finally ended. In the isolation, we had found again the warmth of friendliness that resides in every family, but is sometimes neglected in the work-a-day happenings of every day.

There was one morning in the winter when even the rigours of extreme cold didn't faze one in any way. It was the morning of that wonderful day when I was allowed to go along with Dad and "team" something to town. It might be logs for the sawmill, or wheat for the elevator, or freshly-butchered sides of pork for regular customers who liked to buy their meat in the dead of winter when nature provided natural refrigeration.

I was awake in the pre-dawn blackness, listening intently for the first sound from Father. When I heard a groan, followed by wheezing bed-springs as he swung his bare feet out in search of the wisp of rag rug that protected bare feet from an icy floor, I snatched my clothes and started dressing in the comparative security of the warm bedclothes.

The kindling was snapping in the stove as I came down, and the stove-pipes were just starting to ping as they expanded with the heat. There was a small sifting of snow under the kitchen door. My breath clouded as I helped Father break the thin ice on the water pail and primed the cistern pump. Then there was the reservoir on the stove to be filled, and the pan of milk which had gone into frosty whiskers on top would be placed well back on the stove to melt gently.

This was a morning of such excitement that I didn't want to eat, but was prodded into it with the reminder that it was a long trip to town and back. This was Father's joke. "Better eat up because you won't get anything until we get back."

After the final chores there was the matter of preparing for the trip. It was dead winter, and even when daylight had filtered onto the scene it would still be below zero. I was tucked into an extra suit of underwear. I mean "tucked," because the extra suit was probably one that belonged to my older brother or to Father. Then came two or three pairs of pants, an extra flannel shirt, two sweaters, a smock and a suit coat. Over that I wore an old and rather nondescript fur coat that had shed most of its hair. I put on a big cap with lined lugs over which a woollen scarf was tied, pulled under the chin and then knotted at the back. There must have been four pairs of woollen stockings inside the overshoes that I wore without shoes. Finally, I had to wear home-knitted woollen mitts inside leather pullovers. When Father came up with the team and sleigh I literally waddled out and had to be helped up and placed under the blanket and buffalo robe. Father would wear a cap with the lugs turned down and a great yellow fur coat, with woollen mitts under the leather pullovers.

Then we were off in the half-light. Is there, anywhere, a scene more lovely than that of a frosty winter landscape with light just starting to peep over the eastern rim of the valley? The spruces were like punctuation marks on the white slopes.

The team at first jogged along the track sliced into the snow-covered road by the township snow-plow, and the sound of harness slapping, the squeak of runners protesting on the frosty track, the sloughing sound of the horses' flanks and the jing-a-jong-a-ling of the bells made a most pleasant symphony.

There wasn't much talk, because when we talked Jack Frost knifed at our lungs. Somehow, in all his bulkiness, Father managed to light his pipe and the scent of tobacco smoke wafted at my nostrils. I forgot an earlier and unfortunate experience with tobacco and wished desperately that I was old enough to light up and enjoy a real smoke.

The farms along the way had twinkling lights in kitchen windows and smoke curled lazily in the steely air.

There weren't many sounds, except for the sleigh and horses. As we approached the long swamp, the sound changed with the acoustics of the avenue of elm trees. A rabbit hippety-hopped out from a bush to take an inquiring look at us, and then with an impertinent flip of his cotton-muff tail was on his way. Occasionally we startled a deer nuzzling away at soft bark. Inquisitive dogs came racing down laneways, barking furiously to frighten us on our way.

By the time daylight arrived we were aware that there were other teams ahead of us and some behind us. It was all leisurely. No one tried to pass but each kept a respectable distance from the others. The sound of the different sleighs set up a discordant but strangely pleasant medley.

We travelled on, and because there wasn't much else to do we watched for vacant houses and the Thompson place, where the barn had burned in the fall. In some places there were corn stooks, looking somewhat like tattered Indian wigwams, sitting in the fields. In other places the corn which had been cut looked even more pathetic, the drooping stalks supporting puffs of snow. Father frowned his annoyance. "Some people just don't ever learn to be farmers."

By this time his moustache was icicled and the tufts of his eyebrows were frosty, making him look as if he were a cousin to a frost demon. Before long, I was aware that my nose was running, and I had to start a methodical search for a handkerchief, which was invariably lodged in the inside pair of pants. The pullovers and mitts were clumsy, and so I had to take them off and brave the cold. Having found the handkerchief there arose the problem of sorting out which buttons went into which holes; usually I ended up a sort of crossword puzzle of buttons hitched to the wrong places.

When we arrived at the elevator or the mill, I was deposited in the office, where a kindly secretary offered me cookies or candy. After being in the overheated office for about five minutes, I was uncomfortably aware that rivulets of sweat were forming all over my body. By the time Father came for settlement I was positively bathed in sweat, and as we left the office the air seemed twice as cold.

That trip, however, had a reward. Driving down the main street, I eyed the stores helplessly, inwardly praying that Father might stop. Finally, when I had almost despaired, he turned into the Presbyterian Church shed and fed the horses with the hay and oats he had brought along.

"Guess we can last until supper-time," he announced, and I knew by the twinkle under the eyebrows that he was only fooling.

The ordeal of trying to extricate myself from the protective layers of clothing was more than made up for by the meal in the hotel dining-room. While it was true that the sissified-looking bank clerk who kept making wise remarks to the waitress was obviously amused by us, the glamour of the meal made up for it.

The girl was very pretty, according to my tender standards, after she winked at me. Everything tasted good. It didn't matter if the soup was watery, or the mashed potatoes lumpy and the gravy on the sandy side; that extra scoop of ice-cream she brought and left with a provocative pinch of the arm made up for it.

After getting painfully back in the cocoon of clothes, I waddled back to the church-shed and started on the long trip home as the dusk began gathering in gray folds on the landscape. Father smoked a cigar, and later he whistled or hummed. I guessed he did, because he was humming when I slipped down into the layers of clothing and the arms of satisfied sleep.

3

WINTER ENTERTAINMENT

WINTER CAME DOWN WITH A DARKENING NOVEMber sky that ruptured and spread a fat, white icing over the whole country-side. We knew that we were snow-locked in our Ontario valley until the following March or early April. The days were whirly-go-gig with school and recess time and snowball fights and sleigh-riding, the excitement heightened by the frosty bite of a wind that nipped cheeks and fingers and slipped down a gullet to put a wheeze in the lungs.

Those were the "white days." Others were soft and content, with dripping eaves. Most of them were helter-skelter, windy days with a blizzard that whipped through the naked trees and made the solemn pines stir and scrape in a grumbling way against the side of the building. The fierce wind drove the frothy snow into road cuts until they were full, and covered haystacks and manure piles with hard-packed ripples and rills. Smarting cheeks were stung by it. Those were the days that kept most folks beside their kitchen stoves.

The winter I spent living with my uncle and aunt was high adventure. There was only one minor chore to be done: I had to feed and water the cow kept by my relatives for fresh milk. It was infinitely better than the daily round of chores at home. Evenings during this magical winter were spent crouched like an unobtrusive elf in a darkened corner of my uncle's country store.

The heady wine of my enjoyment came from the conversation of the forum of nail-keg-warmers beside the glowing iron stove that stood between the hardware and the crockery. The regular members of this unofficial group braved even blizzards for their evening relaxation. Big men, with vein-splotched cheeks and hair that never seemed combed, they whisked in the door on the knife-edged wind. With a great stamping and shaking they sat down to thaw out by the stove. Blue clouds of smoke swirled around them from their crusty old pipes that smelled like wet soot.

The conversation was an easy-going one about heifers and stock and the small bits of gossip about women and councilmen and school trustees. It was the daily chronicle of community doings. With an easy tolerance, the young men also listened to repetitious recollections on the part of their elders, who dreamed aloud of their own youth, of trips to cities and work in lumber camps. My uncle kept busy at his counter filling packages with sugar, oatmeal, raisins or Epsom salts from the great barrels and varnished oak bins that tilted out to reveal everything from citron peel to currants. When he looked up at the old clock and chose some accounts to tote up in the privacy of the kitchen where my aunt was darning socks, I knew it was time for me to go to bed.

The bedroom was cold, heated only by a small open grate from the store below. Nevertheless, there was a fascination in wrapping up in a blanket and listening to the fragments of conversation that drifted up. I would try to piece together the half-sentences, and would soon fall asleep, only to half awake as I was dumped in the feather bed. My aunt would make clucking noises of disapproval about my curiosity and repeat a dire warning about a "death of cold."

That country store and the valley it sat in seemed to be a world of its own, especially in the winter-time. The isolation was broken when a team and sleigh came from the Auburn railroad station with supplies and mail, as well as papers that were several days old. From time to time, Sam Chittick would drive his oil tank-sleigh from Wingham, some fourteen miles away, with kerosene for the ordinary lamps, and naphtha for the gasoline lamps that illuminated the front section of our store with great, white splotches of almost antiseptic light. It was a break in the winter when a dry goods "drummer" came in with a hired team and sleigh to spend two days displaying his trunks of wares that included everything from red flannel bloomers to made-to-measure suits.

Radio was destined to cause a great stir on the farm as elsewhere. Opinions about the worth of the "new-fangled" instrument were divided, but "Wee Angie" Macdonald made short shrift of the new device. He listened as a younger member of the nail-keg forum related how his cousin had bought a radio that brought in people talking, and even music. "Wee Angie" expectorated carefully through the broken mica in the stove-front and said, with easy assurance, "It's only a fad. Who wants a radio when they can have a gramophone?"

It was inevitable, I suppose, that Albert should have latched onto the new marvel of communication called radio, hoping to make some money. Albert spent his lifetime trying to find ways and means of escaping manual labour. There is at least one of his kind in every farm community. He laboured harder trying to avoid work on his farm than if he had actually farmed.

While others toiled at seeding, Albert went out selling lightning rods. His six months in insurance practically ruined a reputable company and evidently sent two adjusters to mental institutions. They finally paid him to give it up.

It was following this unsuccessful venture that Albert became involved with radio. He asked my uncle if he could give a demonstration at the store on a Saturday evening. Much to our amazement my uncle agreed, and by the set of his chin my aunt knew better than to argue with him. He simply said, "Anything would be better than listening to that conversation around the stove. I've heard the same stories over and over again for twenty years." A small sign announcing the demonstration was hung along with the sale bills on the back of the account desk, between the cheese cabinet and the whip rack.

On Saturday morning Albert appeared with his helper, another work-shy member of the community. In the middle of the store on the dry-goods side there was a small counter about eight by three feet which was covered with overalls, smocks and sets of heavy woollen underwear called "ganseys." This was my uncle's favourite spot for snoozing during the long, summer afternoons when the farmers were too busy harvesting to come to the store. It was cleared on this occasion for the radio.

That was a great day in my life. The counter was covered with cabinets and gadgets of various sizes and shapes and an enormous goose-necked horn. The batteries sat on the floor. Albert and his help fussed and fidgeted, hooking and unhooking wires and nervously consulting plans. All in all, they didn't appear to know what they were doing.

Ordinarily there were only seven or eight habituées of the conversation circle present on any given night. On this Saturday evening the store was so crowded that I had to bring in all the kitchen and parlour chairs, as well as a supply of egg crates from the storeroom. The women invaded the sacred evening domain and there were children, too. Most people seemed to think they had to buy something, so we were kept busy at the candy counter selling bull's-eyes, sugar-sticks with rings on them, humbugs, licorice plugs and all-sorts.

Albert and his helper seemed to accelerate their preparations about eight o'clock. The crowd was attentive and waiting expectantly. By eight thirty they were growing restless. The children started to wriggle from their parents' knees and women began to chatter. Then the monster came to life with a high-pitched, screeching sound that frightened the children and made them cry. Just as the audience became uncontrollably restless again, the thing would squawk back into life with a hiss, crackle, pop and roar. Then Albert would fiddle with a knob or a wire and it would go dead. People were beginning to move about, and the women were urging their husbands to take them home, when something wonderful happened: we heard a violin playing, quite distinctly, after which a voice announced that we were listening to KDKA, Pittsburgh, Pennsylvania.

It was a thrilling moment, but it didn't last very long. Later on when everyone had gone I heard, from my perch over the grate in the bedroom, the sound of someone who seemed to be preaching. Albert kept yelling about "getting" Mexico. I fell asleep and was given the feather bed treatment, only to be awakened in the middle of the night when the sound of a thousand devils filled the whole place. My aunt woke up, too, and when she saw that it was three o'clock in the morning, she called down for Uncle John to come to bed, OR ELSE, and to tell Albert to go home. The machine was taken away next day.

There is one memory of that evening I'll never forget. "Wee Angie" Macdonald expectorated into the broken front of the stove and paused by the counter to buy a plug of Stag Chewing Tobacco on his way out.

"What do you think of it, Angie?" asked my uncle.

"Wee Angie" shook his head, "She'll never last, Johnny! She'll never last even if she works, because she'll kill conversation. She'll never last."

Having made his pronouncement, he strode out into the frosty snow of the winter night.

But Angie was wrong; she *did* last. That night, in spite of the limited radio reception, saw the beginning of a change in our community. Soon we had a radio in the kitchen with an extension cord and a big horn in the store and for a couple of hours each evening it was switched on. Before long, Saturday evening had become an occasion. "Wee Angie," slightly hard-of-hearing, would arrive at six o'clock to get a nail keg close to the loudspeaker, where he would wait patiently for Foster Hewitt and the hockey game.

It was when I went off to high school the following year that I really became aware of the changes that signified the beginning of a new era. They now plowed the county roads, making it possible to drive home on weekends in the high-wheeled Model T roadster which my father had bought. He equipped it with a box on the back for hauling provisions. The clutch of winter isolation had been broken and as we drove down the concession, we could see the aerials rigged from poles to chimneys.

The men still came to the store after supper, but they were apt now to stay only for a short time. After all, the world had invaded their kitchens and living-rooms and they talked about Amos 'n' Andy and the Fresh Air Taxi Company in as intimate a way as they had discussed the local doings in the pre-radio days.

The radio came also to our home. One Saturday in late fall,

a man in a shiny Gray Dort Touring drove in with a smile on his face. Earlier I had noticed my father hanging around the woodshed and looking down the concession a great deal, as if he expected someone. There was a hint of something in the air, and it wasn't snow.

It was our radio, delivered by Al Walker, the local furniture dealer and undertaker, who had added radios to his inventory. (Albert Davis was selling tractors that year.)

That was a day of great excitement. The aerial was strung out to the old pine tree. The radio was a long, narrow, brown box with three knobs on the front. The loudspeaker was a large, black horn. We took the wet battery out of the car, attached the "B" batteries and waited. Nothing happened. Al Walker fussed, grew progressively redder of face and began to perspire heavily. At supper-time he was still working on the radio.

When we came in to supper, Hank, the hired man, was poring over the blueprints of the set. Our undertaker-radio salesman, who knew Hank hadn't had any schooling, looked at him smugly. Uncoiling himself from the rocking chair, Hank ambled over to the radio and peered at the maze of wires. In a moment he fiddled with something and the set came alive.

That "wireless" changed our lives. Just as it took the regulars away from my uncle's store, it brought the members of our family together. We listened to hockey games, Saturday-night barn dances, and the humour of Amos 'n' Andy. We heard news almost as soon as it happened. Days of isolation, even in the dead of winter, were gone forever from our valley.

In the old days, the snow that kept us isolated on the farm was also the chief source of much of our winter entertainment. It is risking ridicule, in this jet-propelled age, to suggest that a ride in a horse-drawn cutter, on a crisp winter's day, had great charm. Truthfully, though, can the snoring of a fellow passenger, or the sound of the stewardess being friendly over a raucous public-address system, compare with the clear-cut sound of cutter bells?

There was always a fascination about the sound of those bells. They "ting-a-linged" or "jing-jonged," depending on the day or sometimes even the hour. From open stretches of country-side, to the shadowed swamp with its massive pines, elms and basswoods, the music of the bells changed from frosty-clear to deep and resonant.

The cutter runners squeaked and groaned, as if complaining of the frost, while the horses clunked against the dash. The edge of the wind caught at your lungs and put frost whiskers on the edge of your cap. You snuggled deeper under the old bearskin rug and the horse blanket which carried a lingering horsy smell.

I considered myself lucky if I could persuade my parents to let me go on a sleigh-ride with slightly older people. I derived a vicarious thrill from the bundling couples and their stolen kisses. It wasn't Hollywood style, but it was genuine, and some time later in April I pondered on the number of marriages that were taking place.

Too few youngsters to-day can enjoy the delights of skating that the previous generation experienced. Going to the local artificial rink doesn't measure up somehow to the joy of shouldering skates and shovel and trudging down laneways and across fields until you came to the big pond. While some shovelled, others built the raging bonfire. There was the sound of skate blades singing on ice that was, perhaps, not quite smooth. Happy shouts rang past the splashes of light from the bonfire, and went winging up through the night-blue sky with its star freckles. For a brief moment the watching angels must have envied the earth people.

There was even a mild excitement in going into the village and seeing a man plowing the sidewalk with a horse-drawn, V-shaped wedge for a plow. When the snow blew high and piled on the sidewalk I could walk along in the early twilight and peek down from the mounds, in a superior way, at the people in the shops and stores.

It was a world of harsh weather and hardships that created the country person's sense of simple pleasure. We have forgotten the art of finding happiness and contentment in the simple life, and this seems to be the greatest loss to the new generation.

4

THE WORLD OF IMAGINATION

HAVING BEEN RAISED IN AN AGE WHEN EDUCATION WAS hard to come by, my grandfather came, over the years, to depend a great deal on his imagination.

When he was a boy, the schools were primitive, and husky lads were considered of more value working the land than occupying seats in the one-room school. In the country, books and newspapers were scarce, while magazines were practically non-existent.

Thus it was that Grandfather's imagination came into play. In his day, stories of the early pioneer days were passed on by flickering firelight. Itinerant pedlars, barn-framers, apple-packers and horse-traders brought fresh stories as well as old ones with new frills on them. These were the raw materials on which Grandfather's imagination worked.

Conditions had changed by the time we were growing up, but Grandfather hadn't changed a bit. He had little knowledge of reading and the only tunes he enjoyed on the phonograph were jigs, reels and tearful Irish ballads. His greatest enjoyment came from gathering several youngsters around him and telling them stories of his own childhood, and his work in the lumber camps. He also had a fund of fanciful yarns about the spooks and goblins that he claimed inhabited the woods on our place.

One of his favourite stories was about the dance of the rabbits that took place on nights when the winter moon was at its fullest radiance. Grandfather had a great affection for rabbits and in all the time I have known him to hunt, I never saw him shoot one.

I can still see him sitting in the rocking chair, the firelight from the front of the kitchen range spilling over his hair and flickering across his face, outlining the ends of his moustache until they looked like fiery tapers. He took the pipe out of his mouth, opened the front damper, and with a glance to see that my mother wasn't watching, spit into the ashes.

"Ah, yes!" he began. "Rabbits are mighty interesting. They're intelligent, too. You see, there weren't *always* rabbits here. In fact, there were none at all when the first Indians ranged through this country from Georgian Bay, south into what we now call the United States. These Indians lived in wigwams and were a mighty strong people. They had to be, because the climate was very cold and the winters were long.

"Now, the Indians used to catch beaver, fox and mink and use their skins for winter clothes. They used deerskin to make their wigwams. When they had plenty of game to eat and many skins to make moccasins and wigwams with, they were happy.

"One year a great drought came upon this country. It came in the early summer when the corn was starting to leaf out. The dryness withered the corn stalks and shrank the berries on the vines. The leaves of the trees hung limp and the streams started to dry up. Only the Indians who lived close to the Great Lakes were not thirsty, and they could live on fish. As the summer drew into fall the small inland streams, and even some of the rivers dried up to mere trickles. Unable to find food, the animals moved away.

"There were no white men here in those days. The Indians

had never seen a white man. One day, after weeks of drought, a white, or what you call an albino, child was born to a young Indian girl. Everyone was very much afraid and the chief went into his lodge to pray to the "Good Brother" who was the good spirit that helped the Indians. His Indian name was Tijuskeha.

"The Indians had lost hope and were huddled in their wigwams, when a strange thing happened. Snow began to fall. It continued to fall. It continued snowing all night, and all the next day, stopping at dusk. A full moon arose, although it was not time for a full moon.

"The chief told his people that these strange happenings must be an answer from Tijuskeha. The Indians waited. In the middle of the night, when the moon was shining full, they saw some strange creatures come out of the forest. They didn't walk like the fox or the deer or the bear. Instead, they moved with a hopping motion. Their ears were long and their fur was as white as the new snow. They came to the village and began to circle the tent of the girl who had borne the white child. They danced around the tent in the moonlight. They would circle one way and then stop and circle the other.

"At first the Indians were afraid but their chief told them that these animals were the answer of Tijuskeha, the "Good Brother." The next day they set snares for the strange creatures. They found that rabbit's fur made warm clothes and that the meat could be used in the stew-pot. Soon the Indians' fires were burning again. The rabbit broth was bringing life back to the children and the old ones. The foxes and other animals returned. A most unnatural thaw started shrubs and buds blooming, providing medicine herbs for the Indians and food for the returning deer.

"That's how the rabbits came, and no matter how many rabbits they killed for their use, there were always plenty more of them. And here's the odd part of the story. Even nowadays, if you look out at midnight on a night of a full moon to the open field or the space on the front lawn, when fresh snow has fallen, you'll see the rabbits dancing the ring just as they did on that first night in the village on the shore of Lake Huron."

My brother, much older and more skeptical than I, asked why there were brown rabbits now, as well as grey ones; what had happened to the baby, and so on, but Mother rescued Grandfather by sending us to bed.

The imagination unleashed by Grandfather whetted my appetite for books. At that time, books were not considered to be of paramount importance to the majority of rural residents.

The one-room school had a limited library of somewhat tattered and dog-eared books which were kept under lock and key. At some point in the tedium of going to school a teacher asked me one day before Christmas holidays if I would like to take home a book to read during the holiday season. More to please her than anything else, because my heart was set on skating and sleigh-riding during the holidays, I said I would. The book she lent me was *Captains Courageous*.

It stayed with my forgotten school books until we had a blizzard one day. It was a howler that swept down ferociously, followed by a thirty-six-hour stretch of wind that blew the snow into monster drifts and plugged up the concession.

We were truly winter-locked and Mother, with true woman's instinct, started to bake bread. The front parlour, normally opened in the winter-time only for festive occasions or a Sunday evening, was pressed into service with a roaring fire in the heater. I picked up *Captains Courageous* and began to read. Suddenly a new world opened up before me.

There were plenty of things in that book that my mind couldn't comprehend and while my father, being a landlubber, wasn't much help in interpreting, Grandfather willingly supplied the details. When I re-read the book a good many years later I realized that his imagination had been given free rein, and that most of the details were erroneous.

Captains Courageous unlocked the door for me. I must have read it three or four times during the Christmas holidays. Then I went in search of more reading material. Our library was limited to a Bible, a copy of *Home Veterinary Remedies*, *Lives of the Saints* and a pictorial history of World War I. I had looked at the pictures in the latter many times, but hadn't read the text.

I realize now that the teacher was delighted when I went back to school thirsting for more reading adventure. She gave me a copy of *Black Beauty*. It was then I began to encounter some of the old rural prejudices that existed against reading. When I was supposed to be doing chores I was reading. It didn't matter if the room was cold; I didn't notice it. There was general agreement that I was reading too much and would ruin my eyes. One evening the book was taken from me and placed on the clock shelf and I was sent to bed earlier than usual.

I had to wait a long time for the rest of the family to fall asleep. When all was quiet, I crept down the creaky stairs by the dim light of the turned-down lamp in the hallway and took the book back up to bed. Under the covers, reading by the light of a candle, I finished *Black Beauty*; and it's a wonder I didn't burn the house down.

My uncle, the storekeeper, had a liking for books and I discovered he had a small stock of them. This was treasure, indeed. My strongest memories concern a book called *Cast Up by the Sea*. It was many years before I could disabuse myself of the idea that the South Sea natives could smell intruders for miles.

When it became apparent that, like an alcoholic who can always find a supply of spirits, I could find books even when they were prohibited, there was a great deal more tolerance shown to me. To my amazement I received three books for Christmas one year. My uncle gave me an Edgar Wallace mystery, my mother bought me one of the Anne of Green Gables series and my father, for some reason or other, bought me an English annual edited for boys.

There was some doubt about the Edgar Wallace book being suitable for one of my tender years. Father picked it up as I was going to bed on Christmas night. In my bed, immersed by candlelight in the Green Gables book, I realized it was midnight when the clock chimed the hour. It was then I heard Father climbing the stairs to bed. It was the first time, outside of an emergency, I had ever heard him deviate from his regular bedtime of nine thirty.

Books started coming to our home quite regularly after that. My aunt even saved me book sections from weekly papers. I read everything I could get my hands on. I found that Father, rather than spend Sunday afternoon drowsing on the sofa, would read.

One evening while my mother was darning a sock, she asked Father to read aloud. He cleared his throat and stammered that he didn't read very well, but he started at the beginning of *Silas Marner* and read very well indeed. This was a new adventure. Other books followed. It was fun to curl up in the armchair beside the kitchen range and watch the characters come alive in the flames that could be seen through the open damper. Come alive they did, and I can still taste the salt of the tears that fell when Father read about Little Nell.

Even Grandpa, who at first pretended to pay no attention, would let his pipe go out and the ashes slither down his vest, listening raptly. He could be heard muttering dire threats at some of the villains from Dickens who, one felt, were lurking in the shadows of the kitchen at night when the wind strained through the pine boughs on the west side of the house or rattled a storm-window.

Books, in the isolation of our farm, came to be a link with another world of imagination. The three books I had received that Christmas gradually multiplied, until I had managed to build up a whole shelf of them. Exponents of selected reading would have said they were a ragtail and bobtail group, but, from Manuel to Mowgli, they were the closest friends of a young boy in the winter solitude of an Ontario farm.

A simple one, the almanac, was a great source of entertainment for us. I can still see the cover of it, showing the bespectacled and bearded face of Dr. Chase, hanging on the nail beside the newspaper rack whose fancy lettering proclaimed "Home Sweet Home." On evenings when the wind dashed snow against the windows and drifted it against the door, the almanac came in handy.

While Mother was busy darning or mending, Father perused the paper. Grandfather, who was a talker, not a reader, got fidgety. The pungent tobacco smoke curled up through his moustache after he had carefully lit his pipe with a cedar splinter.

"Jenkins is going to sell the red heifer."

Father, intent on the world's happenings, simply grunted.

"She's from that cow he bought two years ago from Ed. That cow was one of the best that Ed ever had."

There was another faint grunt from Father.

"You could stand another cow, and that heifer is due to freshen in March."

Father looked up over his glasses. "He wants too much money for that heifer."

There was an air of finality as he adjusted the glasses, shifted the rocker and went back to his newspaper. Grandpa took the pipe out of his mouth and leaned over to pat old Tabby, who was stretched out on the mat. Then he whistled a nameless tune through his gums and looked up in time to catch me looking at him.

"I think he would be reasonable," Grandpa said, after due pause. "Think he needs the money for a mortgage payment."

Nothing happened. Grandpa got up and went over to the window.

"Sure is a ripsnorter to-night. Bet she goes down below zero."

Then he reached up and unhooked the almanac.

There was silence as he laboriously went through the almanac.

"First quarter of the moon to-night."

That was the opening shot. Mother mumbled something about not being able to see the moon because of the weather.

"Sun rises to-morrow at six fifty-five and sets at five thirty-three."

Painstakingly Grandfather, never too adept at reading, spelled out the detailed forecasts coming up triumphantly to the date.

"Unsettled weather. By golly, it's amazing what those fellas can predict. Better than the weather reports in the paper. Why, do you know they said it was going to be mild to-morrow?"

To Father the newspaper was the lifeline of communication. It was sacred and he devoured it from front to back.

"It said it would be stormy to-morrow," he announced, rising to the bait.

Grandfather had moved on.

"By golly, look what it says. People born between February 19 and March 20 are people of Pisces. It says we're imaginative and like new ideas and are very friendly."

Suddenly he stopped and Father, looking up over his glasses, said, "Well go on! Tell me the rest."

Grandfather turned the page but Father was hooked. Going to the sideboard, he rummaged until he found Dodd's Almanac, which was Mother's favourite, and looking up the horoscope, laughed.

"You forgot to add that it says people in that period lack confidence and are easily influenced by whims."

Then followed the ritual of looking up what the horoscopes said about each of us. Mother laughed when she came to her own. It ran from June 22 to July 22 and said, "Born under the sign of Cancer you are kind and understanding. Choose a job you like to do. Fight against laziness and moodiness to be successful."

We found that Father, born under Virgo, had a logical and precise mind and might have been a good scholar or teacher. Then the sting came when it said that "he must guard against pettiness and coldness."

Mine came under Libra and I found that I was artistic, sensitive and idealistic. I had to be practical to succeed. I had to guard against fickle love distracting my ambition in life. This called for some joshing about Betty Jenkins.

Then they started quoting jokes from the almanac.

Grandpa broke up the party when he read slowly, "Yes, dearie, she says it's the real thing and not just a passing finance." Everybody laughed, but he couldn't see what was funny because "fiancé" was not in his vocabulary.

I went off to bed then with a warm feeling about the family, and I could hear the murmur of their voices as I drifted off to sleep, aware in a dim fashion of the magic of the almanac in bringing us all so close together.

5

LAMPS AND TEAPOTS

YOUNG PEOPLE GROWING UP ON THE FARM WILL not share with us, the older generation, the privileges of the coal-oil lamp and lantern. To them lights mean only flipping a switch while to us the whole problem of illumination was troublesome and complicated.

The first task after the breakfast dishes were finished and the kitchen floor swept was that of cleaning the chimneys on the lamps and lanterns and filling the receptacles with coal oil, or kerosene as it was often called. A five-gallon can of it stood in the woodshed. Some of it was poured into a smaller can for convenience. A woman who failed to have her lamps cleaned and filled in the morning was considered to be a poor housekeeper.

After being cleaned the lamps were lined up like soldiers in new uniforms on the kitchen sideboard. The lanterns were hung in a neat row in the woodshed where they waited patiently for their night duties.

When night came, the lamps were lit and placed in their various stations. The big one with the white bowl that held so much coal oil was placed on the kitchen table. Mother took a small one for use in the pantry. When we went to bed she took another small one and placed it on the table in the upstairs hallway. The last one to bed was supposed to blow out the lamp. That was the signal that the day was over, for our family at least.

That hallway lamp was also tell-tale evidence that Sister was entertaining her beau downstairs or that I was staying out pretty late. If Father woke in the night and the lamp was still lit he would grope for the watch in the bib pocket of his overalls to check the time. Next morning the guilty party would be called upon for an explanation. The trick was either to have a younger brother or sister turn the hallway lamp so low Father couldn't see the hands of his watch, or else have them blow it out. The trouble was that you couldn't depend upon them to stay awake until after Father was snoring in bed.

The lamp in the front parlour was a thing of massiveness if not of beauty. Two enormous globes of transparent pink glass decorated with rosebuds covered the chimney and most of the lamp. It was called into service for Christmas, when we had company, or when Sister was entertaining a beau. No modern miracle of neon lighting could have given us, as children, any greater thrill than the ruddy glow from the rosebud-decorated shade. Mother was constantly reminding my sister that it was indecent to turn it too low on a Sunday evening. I have often wondered if she was as concerned with my sister's morals as she was about what the neighbours might think if they saw only a faint glow coming from the parlour window.

The lights were a signal at all times. Father, lighting the morning fire in the kitchen, always looked across the road to see if the neighbours were up and about. In the winter-time a light in the kitchen was a sign that everything was all right. In the summer-time you watched for a smudge of smoke from the kitchen chimney. Lights in the middle of the night were sure signs of an emergency and somebody would be dispatched to see if help was needed.

Lantern light in the stable cast a friendly and mysterious glow. One lantern hung in the middle of the stable over the cows and Father carried another one with him as he went about the chores. The barn abounded in corners of dark mystery—the empty box stall, the place behind the root pulper or the corner next to the chop box. They were excellent places in the game of hide-and-seek that we carried on when we could escape chores.

On Sunday, if we had been visiting, everybody pitched in to do the chores and all the lanterns were pressed into service. As youngsters, we were given the privilege of carrying them. Milk had to be carried to calves, eggs had to be picked from the nests and the pigs had to be fed. We felt very important, walking in the centre of the glowing pools of light cast by the lanterns, as we walked from the stable to the hen-house or the piggery.

In the late fall when the chickens refused to go into their pens, it was an adventure to get the lantern and help Father pluck them from the limbs of the apple trees where they were sleepily roosting. When Father looked up from his newspaper at night, took off his glasses, put aside the paper and said, "I think there's a weasel at the chickens," all three of us boys raced for the lanterns. He picked up the shotgun, dramatically threw open the breech and slammed in a pair of shells. The breech snapped shut and we were off for adventure.

If we lived with a dangerous fire hazard we were unaware of it. Father taught us that lanterns and lamps were to be used in a certain way. If he caught us fooling while handling either a lamp or a lantern he would administer a good "cuff on the the lugs" that dissuaded us from any more tomfoolery.

We had the best fun of all in the kitchen, which was big and comfortable, with room for the family to spread around. Mother used to knit by the lamplight or darn socks. Father, after perusing the newspaper, sat and smoked by the open oven door. We children explored the shadows that lay beyond the range of the lamp, grateful that we could often escape the sentence of "time to go to bed" simply because of the protection afforded by the inadequacy of the coal-oil lamp.

You can electrify and mechanize and modernize. You can eliminate the coal-oil lamps but you can't banish the old cracked teapot—the source of cream and egg money. Each week the money came in, with seasonal variations caused by the cows drying up or the hens going broody. Nevertheless, it remained the mainstay of steady income. It took care of the groceries, telephone bill and pump repairs, and the balance was tucked into the old cracked teapot on the kitchen sideboard.

The man of the house could scoff and say that the hens were eating their fool heads off when grain was expensive. He could start a campaign to leave the calves on the cows and save the milking, but no matter what a nuisance milking might be, that bit of cash each week was a lifesaver. Of course you couldn't blame a man for complaining when he came home late on a Sunday evening in his best clothes and had to round the cows up from the swale or a dew-laden pasture.

The teapot with the cream and egg money was scrutinized very carefully just before Christmas by Mother. She met the cream man and demanded the envelope before the family could get their clutches on the cash. She took the eggs to town and would not leave the cash balance as a "due bill" for the leaner months when cream and egg production slackened.

Practically every evening found her with the contents of the teapot spread out on the kitchen table for counting. She figured on a sheet of paper, stopping now and then to consult the mail order catalogue. It wasn't that she ordered much from the catalogue, but it was a ready source of vital price information and gift suggestions, as well as being a fount of entertainment.

Not even the promise of a portion of the "pig money" when the next load of porkers was sent to market could extract any loans from the teapot bank. There was a determined set to Mother's jaw as she explained that she was going to finance the Christmas presents on the cream and egg money.

It would be interesting to know how many times that source of cash has saved the average farm family. In our own case, we never knew what the cash resources actually were at any given moment. It was almost impossible for anyone but Mother to find out how much there was in the teapot. The money was interspersed with bills, receipts, coupons and a flock of other treasures.

It was dramatic the way that cash came to the rescue. Tax time came along and Father found himself digging into spare coats and overalls for quarters or an overlooked folded bill in his good suit.

The kitchen table became a repository for stray cash and pieces of smudged paper, staples and odd shingle nails as the search proceeded. Then there was a scramble in the bureau drawers for stray change dumped after a trip to town or church. The shortage was whittled down and then there came a mute appeal to the "Lady of the Teapot." Suspense ran high as she took it from the sideboard. Her fingers deftly flicked through the accumulation of money and apparently useless bits of paper. Out came the necessary money, but without revealing the assets remaining, in the true tradition of a bank. Incidentally, Father always paid back the loan on occasions like that because experience had taught him that you can ruin your credit even with a teapot by not paying your debts.

A good many farmers who had successful places should have been ashamed of themselves when they started boasting about their ability to finance. Many of them depended on their wives to pull them through hard times and emergencies with the cream and egg money. They always knew that no matter what happened, there would be something to tide them over in the chipped teapot or the cracked gravy-boat or the monstrosity of a vase that Aunt Martha had given them for a wedding present.

No matter what you wanted it for, the old teapot always seemed to have the money. I often wondered what a bank manager would have said if Father had given as a credit reference the cracked teapot on the sideboard in the kitchen.

Of course, other teapots still performed their normal functions: Tea was an indispensable beverage on our farm. It seems that over the years our household was laved and bathed in thousands of gallons of tea. The old brown teapot sat on the back of the stove from early morning until late at night, its contents getting stronger as the day wore on.

During the day no one ever thought of rinsing out the teapot and starting over again. As far as my grandfather was concerned the tea only started to get fit for drinking after dinner and it was really something just before bedtime, when it had reached the consistency of lye.

My father, winter and summer, was always the first to get up in the morning. He lit the fire in the kitchen range, put the kettle on, then went to the barn to water the stock. When Mother got up she put the tea in the teapot and steeped it with the bubbling hot water. That was the tea for breakfast and Grandfather always mumbled about its being so weak.

About ten o'clock Father vanished. If you caught him, he always had some pretext or other for a trip to the house. If you followed him, you were certain to find him with a biscuit or a piece of bread and butter and a cup of tea, half-hiding at the back of the reservoir of the old kitchen range. The chances were that he had put more tea leaves in the pot and replaced the water. The teapot was sitting halfway on the fire and starting to boil. Grandfather came in for his cup and poured out a brew that looked like molasses. Then the teapot would be set on the cooler back lids.

By dinner-time the tea was so strong that Mother insisted on diluting it with hot water for the younger members of the family, but Father and Grandfather smacked their lips in sheer delight. About four o'clock in the afternoon, Father slipped into the house and Mother, with a few sticks of kindling, "hotted up the pot." By this time, she had retreated to a small pot of gentler tea for her own consumption.

At supper-time more tea leaves were added and the whole thing given a quick boil. I gave up then and diluted the stuff without any urging, but Father and Grandfather stuck with it. If someone dropped in Father was sure to put a few more tea leaves in the pot and pour a cup for the male visitor while Mother shared the small and milder pot with the lady visitor.

After supper the teapot was filled with water and, in summer-time, placed in the warming closet. The fire went out and it was a favourite pastime to try to sneak a drink of cold tea from the spout. Mother kept up a running battle against this unsanitary sport.

Father set us a bad example because he often tried to drink from the spout, too. When Mother caught him she said, "Tch! tch! How on earth can I bring those boys up to behave themselves when you do things like that?" Father would grin sheepishly and wipe his lips with the cuff of his shirt, saying, "But Ma, it tastes better out of the spout. Besides, I wanted to save you washing a cup."

Strong tea was a requisite of farm life. I have seen Doctor Macdonald, after fighting his way out over the drifted concessions in the winter in a horse and cutter, come stomping into our kitchen and without a by-your-leave, pour himself a full portion of the steaming black liquid, which he drank down as if it were cold water. Then he would straighten up, rub his hands together over the heat of the range and say, "Strong tea is one of the Lord's blessings."

Tea leaves were of use even after they had had their essence boiled out of them. During spring and fall housecleaning they were used to damp down the carpets and keep down the dust. Mother used to throw them in the hen-house because she insisted they kept the hens from scratching, although I don't think it made much difference.

The tea leaves were also a prime source of amusement during the long winter evenings. When Old Meg, a strange, dark woman from the village, came to help out at Christmastime or to act as a midwife, many cups of tea were consumed to hear her read fortunes from tea leaves. Certainly, no nightclub entertainer could have put on a better performance than the strange old woman with the piercing black eyes, as she deciphered the mysteries of the leaves in the bottom of a cup which had been carefully drained and turned three times around on the saucer.

Was there ever anything to compare with the cup of hot, boiling tea from an old pot suspended over a fire in the sugar bush on a day when the sun shone warm but the shadows still had a spring chill in them? And cold tea that had been chilled in an icy spring had a refreshment value on a hot summer day that would put the most highly touted beverages to shame.

6
CHRISTMAS

THE BEST THING ABOUT CHRISTMAS ON the farm was that it began long before the festive day itself came along. Elaborate preparations for the occasion were undertaken with such willingness and attended to with such interest that the happiness of the season was stretched out to relieve some of the bleakness of late autumn days.

Was there ever an event like that of the annual baking of the Christmas cake? Women seemed to wait, like the navigators of old, for good omens or signs before undertaking the task. It could come any time from September until the middle of the week before Christmas.

I always knew the fateful day had arrived when Mother sat at the kitchen table, pencil poised over a flattened-out envelope, perusing the old scribbler. That scribbler contained Mother's secrets and some of them were more precious than life. She kept her recipes in it, but the only time she ever consulted it was when the Christmas-cake baking was at hand. To make ordinary dishes she went by the "pinch of this and sniff of that" method. It was different for the Christmas cake.

The stub of pencil darted down and made notations and Mother mumbled in a sort of trance-like state about "peel . . . citron . . . orange and lemon . . . walnuts . . . hummmm . . . raisins . . . the big ones with the seeds in . . . and currants . . . and some fine blackstrap." There was a pause. "We need sugar . . . white . . . brown . . . icing . . . some of those candied cherries . . . and maybe . . . oh yes, we must have almonds." Then Father was handed the imperial order, with the stern admonition that he hurry, and remember to tell Tim Murphy that "if there is one single thing that isn't fresh we'll go and deal at Crawford's across the street."

On the day of the Christmas-cake baking, I always made an excuse to stay in the house. Soon the kitchen table was littered with papers and flour and baking things. The batter was mixed and stirred to just a certain consistency as the various ingredients were added. There was an occasional pause, as Mother stood and sampled the batter, and then, nodding approvingly, she resumed beating it harder than ever with the big wooden spoon. Eventually, it pleased her chef's palate.

The tin was ready and greased. It was a shining, round milk pan well greased, with a baking-powder can full of shingle nails sitting in its centre.

The moment of the pouring of the batter was a solemn one. Like a dignitary at a cornerstone-laying, Mother smoothed out the batter in the pan. Then she put her hand in the oven to find out scientifically if it were the right temperature. After a slow-burning stick had been added to the fire-box, the cake was gently slipped in to its baking place.

Wild horses couldn't keep me away, when hours later the cake was taken gingerly from the oven. When a cap had been placed on the baking-powder tin, the cake was reverently turned over on a sheet of brown paper. The tin was gently removed and Mother tapped the cake with a forefinger to see if it had any hollow spots. While the intoxicating aroma of spices, nuts and fruit was driving me hungry-mad she pondered over the cake.

I could always tell it was a good one when she looked up

and said, "Dear me, I wish my Christmas cakes would turn out as well as they used to." That was a cue for Father to say, "If you had put some rum in it, you might have had something."

There was a flash of anger as she exclaimed, "You and your smelly old rum. There's not going to be any rum in any cake of mine. I don't want the children to be getting a taste for the vile stuff."

"But didn't you put anything in it?"

Reluctantly she admitted, "Well, I did put a little brandy in it."

To Father, that was always an example of the reasoning of women. Never put rum in it, but brandy won't hurt.

By the time the first snow came the schoolteacher had been reminded by mothers, school children and all the eligible bachelors in the community that they were interested in the Christmas concert. By the first of December, when the snow was usually deep, the poor teacher became aware that in the eyes of the school trustees, the concert ranked next in importance to having her entrance class pass all their exams.

Rehearsals accordingly began during the first week of December. With the wisdom of Solomon, the teacher found a play with as many characters as possible to include all the young people. Since it was imperative that each of the children in the one-room school participate, the result was a mighty long affair.

As the rehearsals stepped up from two a week to every night, the battle reports crackled on the party line. Mrs. Henderson was angry because her Billy had only a four-line recitation and Jimmy Harris was doing a part in a play. Agnes Moore wanted her Milly to play "Humoresque" on the violin. She would have her money's worth out of those violin lessons or else know the reason why, and she couldn't understand the teacher allowing the Jenkins twins to do a harmonica duet.

The part I liked was the sleigh-ride to the schoolhouse. How delicious it was to scrunch down in the clean hay and pull the buffalo robes up to my chin. With a full moon flowing across the white plains of snow and casting shadows from the snow-laden trees and bushes, the world was a wonderful fairyland.

The schoolhouse scene burst at us with the glare of the

hissing gasoline lamps. As usual, somebody had fired the box stove to white heat, and the windows had to be opened. The desks had been removed and crowded down front for the small children, and behind them were ranged the hard wooden fold-up chairs borrowed from the undertaker in the village. Overhead there was a maze of red and green crepe-paper garlands and red bells. Across the front, sheets had been hung from a clothesline. On one side of the room was the organ borrowed from Milly Simpson, who taught music. On the other side, in the corner, and dominating the whole room, was a monster Christmas tree standing two feet deep in parcels, crowned with a somewhat bedraggled tinsel star at ceiling level.

Everybody talked out front and giggled behind the curtain. We got an occasional glimpse of an eye peeking out from a tear in one of the sheets. Ab Crich, after a whispered conversation with the teacher and Milly Simpson, called for order. A somewhat ragged version of "God Save the King" opened the concert.

Each parent was waiting expectantly for his or her child's part in the concert. This meant an almost uniform amount of applause for each act. We had angels and black-face artists and "rube" acts and singers and sometimes a jig or two. The time passed until the *pièce de résistance*—the play—was reached. Then Ab Crich stood up and over the sound of the chairs thumping and sets being moved behind the curtain, he made his address.

Ab praised all the school children who assembled out front. On cue he stopped talking and Milly broke into a "show tune" like "Silver Threads Among the Gold" and the curtain was pulled back jerkily along the knotted clothesline. The show was on.

I remember one year when George Hendry was sitting on the settee that had been borrowed for the occasion from the manse. He was wearing the one decent pair of false whiskers in the district. George droned on about the price of wheat and the weather and the trouble he was having with a beau who was courting his daughter. Then the catastrophe happened. His whiskers dropped off. George was a good actor. He just went right on talking and said, "Yes, sir, times are tough. There hasn't even been enough rain to help a man keep his whiskers stuck on."

There were several mishaps. Part of the curtain that

served as the girls' dressing room fell down and showed Emily Smith in her knickers as she was changing her dress. She blushed steadily for a month after that. Tom Dickson's stomach slipped and he split a shirt button, so that we could see the pillow ticking. Emily Lawes froze on her lines and finally the coach said in a loud whisper, "Clear out your ears, Emily," whereupon she went off the stage and had to be coaxed back for her part.

When Mary Joe McLaughlin and Peter Sims "clinched" in the final scene it was so realistic that Eddie Joe Fisher, her boy-friend, was halfway to the stage before it broke up. Most people thought it was too realistic.

Towards the end, the blacksmith came as Santa Claus and the presents were distributed. There was a round of applause for the teacher, who blushed her thanks for all the co-operation she had received. Finally, just after midnight and four hours of concert, we started for home. The men scrambled for their coats and went to the shed for the sleighs and cutters. Most of them spent a fair time in the shed and the wives were starting to get anxious before they appeared.

I noticed on the way home that there was singing on the part of the men and mumbled anger on the part of the women. There was something about "cider" and "disgraceful," but as a youngster I didn't pay much attention, huddled in the comfort of the sleigh and watching the heavens dimpled with bright stars. The memories of the warmth and companionship flooded into my heart. It was a moment when I felt good about myself and the people I lived among. Even the memory of the scolding I had received at supper-time for not stripping the red heifer didn't seem to matter.

Later on in bed, I heard the old house settle down, and as the warmth of the stoves oozed out, the frost crept in to make the place creak like a phantom schooner on a moon-white sea. It was warm in the old feather ticks and sleep crept over me as I thought about what I might get for Christmas.

No other day could compare with Christmas Day. It started when I awoke in the morning. The refuge of a feather tick, which on ordinary days was a welcome insulation against the tingling cold of the bedroom, became a sort of jail on Christmas morning. The house was so still. I listened and listened, cold air nipping at my ears as I peered out, but there were no sounds except the frost cracking and the swishing, metallic coldness of pine branches scraping on clapboard. The silence of the house was maddening.

If I went downstairs it would probably waken Mother, who would order me back to bed. Besides that, the house was mighty cold, with the fire in the kitchen stove burned down to ashes. I wondered if I might drop a book on the floor and waken Father. He had threatened to sleep in, but he could hardly have slept much longer. After all, it must have been six o'clock. He usually started the fire at five thirty.

It was pleasant to think about the day that was coming. The stockings would be draped across the rocking chair, plump and bulging, and there would be a big orange at the top of one of them and perhaps a picture-book peeking out of the other. They were the longest stockings in my possession. It had taken a lot of will power to keep from hanging up a pair of Grandfather's lumberjack stockings. There was always a faint hope that big stockings might increase the hoard of presents from Santa Claus.

Did I believe in Santa Claus? At one time I suppose there had been an unthinking faith in the old fellow with the whiskers. Overheard conversations and a lot of other things weakened my faith, but native cunning prevented me from saying a word. It was better simply to go along with the grown-ups than to challenge the one opportunity for presents of a much gayer nature than the practical ones of a birthday.

The morning came alive when Father, protestingly, made his way down to the kitchen. Then I pulled on my clothes in the warmth of the feather ticks, fumbling around in the attempt to get dressed. It resulted in some mishaps but there was always plenty of time before I heard my mother stirring in the wake of Grandfather who had followed Father to the kitchen.

Every year there was an argument about the opening of the presents and the stockings. This ceremony was supposed to happen after breakfast. Father and Grandfather vanished and I sat eyeing the stockings while Mother set the table.

"What could that long, flat thing be, halfway down in the stocking?"

I surreptitiously tried to squeeze the toes. It seemed to be the shape of a jack-knife. It couldn't be! Mother was dead set against me having a jack-knife. There was a rolled-up colouring book in one stocking. The box wrapped in tissue paper on the floor had me baffled.

Breakfast was over in record time. At least it was over for me, but the grown-ups took a terribly long time to eat theirs. Mother looked up with a sympathetic smile, and said that I could open the stockings.

The contents of the stockings varied from year to year and yet there was a great similarity as well. Nuts of all shapes, from peanuts to Brazil nuts, rock-hard candies with gaudy stripes of green and red, and a small package of cream candies, almost cloyingly sweet. There would be a big orange and some figs, two or three pencils and a workbook, a colouring book and a pair of mittens, sugar-stick candy with rings. There was never any gum. I learned in later life that it was Mother, not Santa Claus, who objected to chewing gum.

I wondered how Santa Claus put a wooden boat that looked suspiciously like the one Grandfather had been carving, into my stocking, and how one year he brought the pocket knife and chain that I had looked at so longingly in the store. One year there was a great treat, a wooden stable that had real windows and doors with stalls inside, and a team of wooden, dapple-grey horses pulling a farm wagon. I guess that was the biggest "store-bought" present I ever received, with the exception of the toboggan which I knew my aunt had brought from the city.

The folks opened their presents after Father had put a match to the wood in the front parlour heater. While the stove-pipes tingled with expansion, the parcels were opened. Father received a sweater coat, some red bandanna handkerchiefs, home-knitted mittens, socks and occasionally a tie while Mother received aprons, sweaters, handkerchiefs and stockings and other personal items of clothing which were looked at quickly and bundled out of sight. Grandfather received his usual quota of tobacco, a pipe, or a scarf. Sometimes a city relative sent him a bottle of liquor. Those were the Christmases he enjoyed most.

The day is one of warm, fragrant memories. To read and munch candy, to look at the popcorn balls on the tree, the fuzzy green and red garlands, the tissue paper bells and the glinting silver star on the top of the tree was a delight. There was a lazy quality about the day, especially when fat snowflakes began to slither down outside.

We went to relatives for Christmas dinner. It was a sleigh-ride with bells "jing-jonging," and a great welter and confusion of voices and laughter when we arrived. Shy cousins soon made up over toys, shortly fell out over possession and finally rejoined friendship in a stuffed, drowsy atmosphere of eating and near unconsciousness on the hearth. Sleep came among the robes and blankets of the sleigh on the way home.

Christmas Day, which had started out so tingling and alive with frost and cold, ended in unreality, with the luxury of carefully wrapped bricks and irons taking the chill from the feather ticks. The night was filled with dreams about fat old men with white whiskers who carried toys and sugar candies that danced and went sprawling into a welter of snow that exploded into a cascade of glistening white.

Christmas was always like that. It was so eagerly awaited, enjoyed and then sent on its way. There was a flavour of unreality about the whole thing. In that way it stood out from all other days of the year for a small boy on the farm.

7

JANUARY AND SICKNESS

JANUARY WAS ALWAYS A STRANGELY FASCINATING month in the country. I built anticipation up to a pitch for Christmas. New Year's was a hazy recollection of staying up very late, of red-faced grown-ups discarding their usual country shyness and kissing each other extravagantly. I tried to stay out of reach of the somewhat blubbery lips of a virginal spinster aunt who seemed to enjoy the occasion with a certain abandon.

The days of holiday progressed into the slow tedium of living and work. My folks, accustomed to the ordered ways of country living, seemed to be resting up. Heads nodded sooner than usual after supper in the comfortable warmth of the kitchen.

Somehow or other, I associate sickness with January. Some

person or animal always seemed to succumb to the lonely cold of the month. Those were days when a skittery, cold wind basted hummocks of hard-packed snow. It was a time when the knife-edged wind poked through the cracks of the barn, leaving pencil lines of snow on the brittle hay in the mows.

The barn cats half-hibernated in the stable and the dog had icicles on his hairy coat as he waited to dodge into the warmth of the kitchen. The hens huddled like feathered balls on their roosts or among the damp straw. They waited patiently for us to melt the icy sheath on the water in the assortment of tins that were fore-runners of modern drinking fountains.

January, as I now remember it, seems always to have been a month of snow-clogged roads and crisp, frosty days when Grandfather carried dangling icicles on his moustache as he came into the kitchen from the outside. It was a time when I could ramble across wind-packed, white fields and make fresh tracks. The only footprints ahead of me would be those left by the rabbits doing their strange dances, performed as I was told by Gramp, under the light of a full moon. I could almost believe, in the cold unreality of January, that rabbits were really only pixies or little people in disguise.

A sort of frigid magic pervaded the month. At night I would sometimes creep out of bed and scrape the frost from the window with my fingernails, and peek out at the tableau of trees and buildings edged in black and white. There was always a cold, hard moon. It wasn't unfriendly; it just seemed to be startlingly white, like a big, round diamond, in a setting of blue velvet. The lights from the windows of the neighbours, pale and yellow, would wink out one by one, leaving the white, frozen stretches of field to the staring moon and the enchanted rabbits.

There came, inevitably, an evening when my father was late for supper. He stood hesitantly inside the door, on the old rag mat, with the lantern in his hand. Mother, moving to the stove where the dinner waited in the warming oven, looked up.

"Something the matter?"

This was not a scold for being late. It was an instinctive note of concern for anything which hindered or impaired the regularity of our daily living. Father roused himself, hung up his cap, flicked the lever that elevated the lantern chimney and blew out the flame with a gust of breath. I can still smell the burned wick and kerosene.

"The red cow's not too well."

Gramp, who maintained vital animal statistics on a binder twine "calendar," adjusted his spectacles and walked over to the cellar door. Mother didn't frown. (She had argued against the enumeration being kept in the kitchen. A compromise had been reached by hanging the calendar on the back of the cellar doorway.)

"Flossie's due about now."

Father nodded as he took off his smock, hung it on a peg under the magazine rack, and started rolling up his sleeves preparatory to washing.

"I'm afraid she's in for a tough one."

Sex was not a mystery to a growing boy in the country. Anyone who had ever trudged three miles, tugging on the end of a rope a frisking, romantic cow that wanted to dally with every steer she saw, knew the purpose of the trip and the necessity of the bull, not to mention the futility of a relationship with a steer. This knowledge was further reinforced by men who didn't bother to couch their conversations in polite terms just because small boys happened to be listening. Most of us had at one time or another encountered older boys and girls, sweating and straining, in some sort of romantic exercise, in berry patches or under buffalo robes on a sleigh-riding party. We also knew that when, after a hastily-arranged marriage, a young couple had a baby in nine months or one month, it didn't happen because of a miscalculation on the part of the stork.

Talk was short at the supper table.

"Going to call the vet?"

"I'll see after supper."

Animals were valuable on a farm. A sow that killed her young by rolling on them caused a loss. A cow that bloated on new grass and died meant a capital loss. If a freakish storm let loose lightning bolts, killing animals in a pasture field, we lost a part of our operation.

When there was trouble in the air, Father changed his pattern at the supper table. Usually he pushed back from the table and savoured, with an almost sensual pleasure, at least three cups of tea. This night he spilled milk into the cup and gulped the cooled brew. His place was in the stable. I was usually allowed to go with him. The care of a sick animal was something to be learned. It was part of the unwritten education of a farmer's son.

A January stable by night had a special feeling. Bright, agate eyes gleamed through slits as the barn cats awakened from their sleep on top of the sacks in the chop bin. There was a smell of manure and dry hay, mingled with the lingering odour of the roots that had been mangled in the root pulper. The horses alternated their standing legs like onlookers at a performance that has gone on too long.

When an animal was sick, there wasn't as much noise in the stable as usual. The other animals seemed to sense the difference. Maybe nature had a special form of sympathy of its own. Pups and kittens were not concerned, but the cattle seemed imperceptibly to change their rhythmic pattern of cud-chewing.

The sick cow, helpless in its plight, unable to communicate, stared with dull eyes at us, mutely pleading for help. Even the most belligerent of beasts abdicates resistance in favour of mute appeal.

Gramp knew, when he saw the red cow. He nodded.

"That one lost her first calf."

Father was patting and petting the swollen belly.

"I'd sell her if she pulls through. Must be somethin' wrong with her."

Father didn't seem to hear.

"Flossie," he said, as if the animal could understand, "I think we'd better get some help for you."

It was a strange thing. Father, who would not hesitate to "whang" the head of a balky animal with a two-by-four, always spoke in a gentle tone to the same animal if it were sick or helpless.

"Poor Doc Lindsay," shivered Gramp, remembering other nights. "I don't know how the hell it is that they always get sick when it's either brass-balls cold or storming."

The vet was an important member of any farm community. Doc Lindsay was a big, slow-moving man with a red face and a tattered moustache that looked like a well-worn straw broom. He invariably had a cold stub of cigar in his mouth, but you could tell he sometimes smoked it because of the stains on his moustache. In the summer-time he travelled with a horse and buggy. The small black bag on the seat didn't balance him, so the buggy had a bad list to the right. In the winter-time he travelled by horse and cutter, wrapped in an enormous horse-hide coat, and wearing a black fur cap.

Doctor Lindsay was short on small talk. He was profane and short-tempered and it was generally thought that he had more feeling for animals than for human beings. He worked fifty weeks of the year, seven days a week, twenty-four hours a day. For the remaining two weeks he vanished with his hound, a creature that reportedly slept the rest of the year. He was supposed to be hunting, but most people said he was too kind-hearted to shoot anything.

All the things that people said about the vet came to my mind as we trudged through the snow to the house, stepping in and out of the swinging ring of light from the lantern.

There was a note of definite purpose in Father's tone of voice when he picked up the receiver.

"Tilly," he said, "I want the phone. Cow's sick."

Tilly, an elderly lady of the township who spent a great deal of time in idle chatter on the phone, knew better than to argue.

"Doc, the red heifer is sick, the one that lost her calf last year. Can you come?"

It was as simple and straightforward as that. There were no apologies for the weather. It was Doc's job. He didn't suggest a home remedy. Doc Lindsay knew that my father wouldn't call unless it was absolutely necessary.

It was the same with Mother. She didn't ask what had to be done. The kitchen range was stoked up. The big kettle was shoved forward on the front lids. The tea-kettle was put on because Doc would appreciate three or four cups of scalding, strong tea of the consistency of black lye.

Then it was a matter of waiting. As I peeked out of the window I knew that everyone on the concession was also waiting. Even the telephone didn't ring for a while. When it did ring it was Joe Jim Davis from the bridge to say that he had helped Doc through the big drift in the cut. Father went out to the stable. Gramp stayed for the vet.

Mother poured the hot water on the tea when we heard the cutter bells. Gramp rode down to the stable with Doc. I took the other lantern and went down to pull the horse and cutter into the driving-shed out of the wind.

That's the way the night of vigil started. It was thus I

learned the mystery of birth. It was associated with pain and unpleasantness, and yet the sight of a wobbly-legged calf being gratefully licked by the mother now seemingly recovered, was a picture that stayed with me. The warming sense of relief that pervaded the kitchen at three o'clock that morning, and the old vet sitting, sipping from a great mug of scalding black tea, are other memories.

One January afternoon, I almost didn't make it home from school. I felt odd, and a shouldering wind crowded my footsteps in the sleigh tracks. My head was suddenly hot and then I started to get chilly. At times, when the wind blew gusts of skimpy snow, all the world went white. I stopped then to blink, and a pinkish scene took the place of the white vision, and I stumbled on for another few steps.

I remember falling, and the sound of cutter bells. It seemed as if the horse were going to trample me, and when I tried to scream my throat was raspy and no sound would come out. Everything was in circles. After a long time I could hear voices, but they would come close and then trail away like echoes—maddeningly far away—until they faded out.

My mother had her hand on my forehead and it felt cool. The pale, yellow glow spread out in a circle from the lamp on the old dresser. Father's face seemed to be hanging in midair with no body attached, and my mother kept saying, "There, there now! The doctor will soon be here."

From the face that hung in the shadows I heard a voice say, "It's drifting badly—I'm going to take the team and meet the old doctor."

Mother looked up to the face, which seemed to be fading.

"Be careful now, it's a dreadful night for poor Doctor Jamieson."

Then I was gone again, winding down circles that seemed to widen out and out and I was falling. I swam up to the surface suddenly and abruptly, and I couldn't move at all. A face covered with gray whiskers was looking at me. Then I saw the eyes and made out the face with the small spectacles perched on the nose.

"Pretty sick, boy?"

It was infuriating being unable to say anything in reply. I tried and tried, but red sheets flashed in front of my eyes, turning to orange and it was like fireworks.

"There now, boy. Just lie easy."

I could feel his hand that felt as smooth as my mother's touch my forehead. Then he picked up my wrist. Something gleamed in the lamplight and I couldn't make out what it was, but I could hear ticks and they were as loud as the old clock in the kitchen. Then the house shook and I was away again, falling into snow that was hot instead of cold.

They said I babbled for three days. The first thing I remember is the sun shining in the window and Mother standing beside the bed, near the man with the whiskers.

"Mother! Mother!"

She was beside me then, with a hand on my forehead.

"Mother, I'm hungry."

"Yes, yes, dear."

"Mother, can I have some pancakes?" I said, and it was easy to talk. Then I added, "With lots of maple syrup."

The whiskers erupted into a great, booming laugh.

"Your boy is getting better."

That was my introduction to Doctor Jamieson. He had saved me from pneumonia and I learned later that, when a flu epidemic closed the school for seven days, he had worked around the clock, for stretches of seventy-two hours at a time.

After that when I met him on the street in the village he would stop and ask me how I felt. It was like being admitted to a club because his trips down the main street to the post office were punctuated by little chats with his patients. For the first time in my life I had an ambition apart from being a farmer like my father. I was going to be a doctor like Doctor Jamieson.

I listened to every story that was told about him. He had performed operations on kitchen tables, had walked seven to ten miles through snow, and had once swum a stream in a March flood to save a woman during a difficult childbirth. He never sent bills and he was poor. He never married because he said being a doctor's wife was no life for a woman.

On the anniversary of his fiftieth year of graduation, a celebration was held for him at the township hall. They gave him twenty ten-dollar gold pieces and a handsome new bag with his initials on it in gold. When we were leaving that night I heard someone say, "You know, the old doctor has never been the same since he went through that flu epidemic. There's a young doctor coming to help him."

All the way home I couldn't help feeling guilty. It seemed as if my own sickness had contributed to his ill health, or whatever it was that was wrong with him. I vowed then that I would never go to that new doctor.

People, like all things in this life, change. Two months later we stood and heard the Presbyterian minister eulogize the old doctor. Six months later young Doctor Macleod took out my tonsils, and after the sore throat which preceded the operation, I was glad that he was in our village.

8

MEMORIES OF NIGHT

WHEN I WAS IN THAT STAGE OF GROWING UP, half boy and half man, I shared an experience with grown-ups that left an indelible impression on me. Relatives and neighbours whom I thought I knew so well stood out in a different way. It was as if they were suddenly thrust under a magical probe that disclosed things I had never known.

It happened in early evening after a thawing spring day when the sun was warm and the wind chilly. By night-time, the world had tightened up with a cold, scrawny wind and the kitchen was most comfortable. I had been reading. My mother, father and grandfather seemed to be in a trance as they listened to a musical programme on the radio. There was a good fire, the cat was stretched out asleep behind the woodbox and Mother was gently humming. It seemed to be a scene that nothing could disturb.

The telephone carved through the peace with the blatant sound of our number. Three longs! Two shorts! Father went to answer it. He said very little. There was an ominous note in his voice as he said, "We'll meet you at the cross-roads in ten minutes. No, make it fifteen." When he came back into the circle of lamplight, Mother asked him, alarmed, "What's the matter?"

"The little Williams boy is missing. They thought he was at the grandparents but he wasn't there."

Grandfather stood up but Father motioned him to sit down. He nodded to me, "Better wrap up warm and bring the lantern."

My mother started to protest, but there was no time for argument. She kept fussing around as I dressed. Grandfather made a lukewarm suggestion about going in my place but Father again shook his head. This was the first time he had ever indicated I might be big enough to handle a man's responsibility. He had never objected to my doing a man's work, however. I wanted to tell Mother to stop fussing with my scarf but I couldn't say anything.

When we were out of range of the light from the kitchen windows my father took the lantern and I noticed then that he had his shotgun.

"Now look, lad," he said, "You stick beside me and no nonsense. Somebody saw two tramps getting off the freight in the village at noon. There just might be trouble and I don't want you getting hurt."

The clouds were helter-skelter in the sky. The moon was a crescent lying on its back. The wind was scampish, as if it were playing hide-and-seek, flitting away behind trees or hedges and then coming out to smack us coldly. The road was firm, but not frozen, although there was a rim of ice on some of the puddles that tinkled when we stepped on it.

This wasn't a pleasant stroll down a country road with my father. I sensed more and more strongly the grim determination in his step, and felt his silence, cold as the night wind. There were moments when, almost breathless from our fast gait, I longed for the warmth and security of the farm kitchen.

There were twenty-five or thirty people at the corner. Lantern lights could be seen flickering down each of the roads as more people hurried towards the scene. Talk was in barely audible whispers. Finally Tom Patterson, the township constable, asked for silence.

"The boy is five and he's wearing a mackinaw and a red sweater cap. He was last seen heading for his grandfather's about two o'clock. When he didn't come home his folks called."

A hoarse voice interrupted and I could see it was Pete Williams.

"Ethel and me thought he went to her folks next road over, but when he didn't come back we called just after supper-time and they hadn't seen him."

Light talk rippled among the men. Tom Patterson went on with his instructions. I didn't hear them. Somebody mentioned that they were dragging the river and it frightened me. Shaking my shoulder, Father brought me back to reality.

"Come on, lad, we're going with these fellows. We'll spread out and head towards the river."

About ten of us climbed the fence and fanned out across the Barclay place. The fence wire hummed in the wind. The field was muddy under a crust of cold, hardened soil. The lanterns winked like lightning bugs. It was lonely as we trudged along.

Father was about ten feet from me. Now and again he spoke in a voice that seemed to come just to my ears and stop dead.

"Keep a sharp eye out, lad."

It was comforting, although he was only saying it to keep my spirits up. Maybe he felt the loneliness of the night, too. Somewhere that little boy was alone, cold, perhaps dead. The thought was shivering inside me when a great flaring light went up in the Barclay laneway.

We hurried towards it hopefully.

"Dad?"

"Yes, lad?"

"Maybe they found Joey."

"Maybe."

He didn't sound as if he really meant it. After a trudge of a few minutes he spoke again.

"Joey. Is that the boy's name?"

I answered and the thought came to me that no one had mentioned his name before. It was strange. They had just said it was the Williams boy who was missing. I could see him.

He was a little tadpole who used to play in the front yard of the house that old Joe Willie Williams, his grandfather, had built near his son's after the latter had married. Mrs. Williams had pale golden hair. She was really pretty. As we walked on I tried to remember her face. I couldn't.

Then we heard shots. We were coming closer to the bonfire and the men standing around looked like a tableau in a history book. The bonfire flared up and their faces were stern, golden masks.

"They found the boy," said Ed Barclay.

It was strange how we all seemed to freeze into the tableau beside the fire. The pause was long.

"It was the creek," said a stranger.

"The strangers?" asked my father.

"Never left town," said someone else, "Got a job at the sawmill."

Others were converging from all directions. You could tell it by the increasing light of the lanterns. The men seemed to move of one accord to go home. I wondered why, and then remembered that Mr. Williams might be with them. Maybe they didn't want to see the body which someone was bringing up the sideroad in the doctor's car.

My father scarcely spoke on the way back. We stopped at the kitchen door and with a lack of reserve which I had never found in him before, he put his arms around my shoulders. His voice was gentle.

"Better try and get some sleep, son. If you're tired in the morning don't get up."

I didn't want hot cocoa. I only wanted bed but sleep was a long time coming. When it did it was troubled and full of swirling dark water and swaying lights in a void of silence. Somehow I grasped that night the responsibility of being a member of a man's world.

It was appropriate that an experience such as growing up should happen at night. In the country, night was always a mysterious thing.

I used to like the soft, early summer evenings when I could almost feel a velvet cloak around me. It flowed against me. If I put my hand out I could sense and feel it. A harmonica playing at the neighbours' came over as if the notes were swimming in thick air. A calf bawled in the barn while the frogs tried out their pipes in the swale. These were the humid nights when the earth absorbed the moisture, awaiting the strengthening sun of the lengthening days.

The night, no matter what the season, always contained the sound of a hound baying in the distance. I tried to imagine that the lamplight from the kitchen windows was a flickering campfire on the bald prairie. You could make it seem real when you slitted your eyes and let just peeps of light filter in. The hound was really a coyote. The harmonica came from a lonely cowboy camping out for the night. Night brought me a feeling that lay somewhere between happiness and loneliness.

Always on the farm I could sense and feel the night. It had dark arms that felt like dew in the spring, a warm embrace in the summer-time, a cool caress on sharp autumn nights and a firm, cold grasp in the winter-time.

The sky always had a great effect on me in the night. It was eerie to walk down a deserted sideroad where jutting rail fences made dark patterns of mystery, broken by the winking incandescence of fireflies. On a black night I walked on the edge of fear, trying bravely to whistle away my nervousness.

I remember the night when the sky stood out behind little, cold grey clouds. I was in a cutter or sleigh; on the frost-laden air could be heard the sounds of bells. They were small tinkly bells, and they seemed, in sound, to nod to each other and then respond again, until the whole air was filled with the vibrating harmony. So long ago and far away, the pleasant sound of bells still comes to me sometimes.

I loved the drowsy sound of conversation on porches in the night. The squeak of an old rocker or the slow sound of a swing was the perfect background for a conversation that sounded as good tobacco smells. Walk down a side street in a village sometime, when the moon has been obscured by a passing wraith of cloud, and hear the wisps of quiet conversation. Put in the background the sound of the cricket and the low murmur of traffic in the distance and you have a concerto that has yet to be written.

Have you ever caught the scent of a strong old pipe in the middle of the night? Probably a very old man has risen from his bed, taken his pipe and lit it. Creep into the lee of an aged man who is wondering what he should have done with his life and trying to equate it with what he has done, and you will gain for yourself a lifetime of experience. The sound of the rocker on the uneven boards of the veranda, the sucking sound of the pipe and the wheeze of an old man's chest, all against the background of night, is something that you can never forget—nor should you.

There are so many things to remember about the night!

I remember the swaying yellow flicker of a lantern on the way to the barn. I remember the old-witch clouds scurrying across the face of the moon on a late October night.

Night was sometimes hard and graceless. Although it often had the soft, velvet touch of a spring zephyr, it was sometimes cold and harsh, stinging my cheeks vengefully. Yet even in those moments when the night lashed at me, there was a grace which the day lacked.

I remember a gusty, chilling fall night. We went to bed with the wind moaning in the big pines outside the bedroom windows and the clouds like black ships across the moon. It was a scary night in the season of Hallowe'en when the trees were naked, the harvest over and the potatoes dug. Winter and frost were expected any time. I went to bed with the blankets over my head to shut out the cries of the wind and the pattern of light and blackness thrown on the moon by the wind-driven clouds.

I woke up with a scare at the sound of squeaking boards, and yelled because there was a figure outlined against the window. It was only Father, who said, "Come here, boy, and see." There was a lurid glow in the eastern sky, dying at one instant and then flaring again.

I can still hear my father say, "That must be McAllister's place. Poor Johnny, and him without his threshing done."

"They were threshing there when we came from school," I said, and my father nodded.

If the sight of the reflection in the night sky was terrifying, then the sound of the constant ringing on the party line was the clincher as far as fear was concerned. In the middle of the night when the whole country-side is asleep, the sound of a telephone can only mean sickness, fire or death.

The household awoke in a stumbling hurry and Father, who ordinarily left party-line listening to the women-folk, had the receiver to his ear listening.

"Sure enough, it's the McAllister place," he yelled, replacing the receiver.

At any other time it would have been amusing to see Father stuffing a voluminous nightshirt into his trousers and getting his boots crossed up, or hearing the hired man demonstrate his ability to cuss when his shoelaces snapped.

At first there was a half-hearted attempt to make the children stay at home but in the end we all managed to go along. The older children had to get pails from the milk-house while the hired man brought gunny sacks from the granary. The black drivers were hitched to the democrat and off we went, with Father driving and the hired man holding the lantern. We crouched in the back and Mother clutched our baby sister in her arms. The baby was the one who seemed to be getting the most enjoyment out of the trip. No one spoke, and as we turned off the concession onto the sideroad the reflection in the sky kept getting bigger and bigger.

There were people on horseback and in every kind of rig all heading in the same direction. Some people were walking or running along the road, and everybody was mad when George Fisher came along honking his horn in his new Model T. Coming over the top of Dolan's Hill we could see the barn outlined in flames down in the valley. The flames were flickering out of the open doors and edging between the cracks of the siding. The roof was still intact.

When the team had been tied to the fence, Father and the hired man grabbed up the sacks and pails and ran for the fire. We could see a line of men in a bucket brigade hauling water from the little creek that ran south of the barnyard, in an effort to save the driving-shed. Another group with wet gunny sacks put out sparks on the pigpen roof. Still others were on the roof of the house but it seemed to be safe.

In the hollow of the valley there didn't seem to be as much wind as on the high land. The men were working and the women and the younger children huddled up beside the house. They weren't talking. There was a sort of heavy silence, broken only by an occasional whimper from a baby and scattered talk.

"Well, they got the cows out."

"They're trying to get the horses out."

Then we heard the frightened whinnying of horses. In the stable door we could see men pulling on halters as two big

Clydesdales seemed to fill the lurid, smoky doorway. Suddenly there was a great confusion as the horses, just on the doorstep, bolted back into the stable. It was at that instant that the wind played a prank, gusting over the valley. The fire spurted out like flames on a gas burner. It licked hungrily at the roof and then there was a tremendous sound like a great "pop" as the flames burst through and leaped upward into the sky.

The crowd sighed of one accord and then there was a scream of terror for the men in the horse stable. A man darted to the door shielding his face with a gunny sack and then two men lurched out of the door. One of them was on fire and the bucket brigade broke as two men rushed to throw water on him. It was the owner, Johnny McAllister. The heat was getting more intense and shortly after the men by the driving-shed had been forced farther back, the wind veered around, saving the driving-shed.

To this day I can hear the sound of those horses and see the sides of the barn disintegrating, leaving the ribs of framework. It was like looking into a sort of hell. It flared and burned and suddenly one end of the roof sagged. Finally it fell with a force that sent sparks and flames spouting wildly into the sky.

At that moment the wind died and there were some spitting raindrops. When the rain did come it seemed as if it were to be just another source of irritation. Buckets of tea appeared from the kitchen and for the first time, I was aware that my mother had brought a great jar of muffins. The men, with blackened faces, stood in little knots, drinking tea and eating cakes and muffins and saying very little.

To me the most tragic sight of all was Johnny McAllister sitting in a rocker on his veranda, his hands covered with white bandages, staring at the fire, while his wife stood beside him equally silent with her hand on his shoulder.

We drove home in the chill of a cold, black morning. It had been a night of excitement but the kind of excitement that leaves a numbing feeling inside. Even the next day on our way to school, when we saw smoke curling up from the blackened ruins there was nothing we could think of to say to each other. It was a big relief when young David McAllister came out of the laneway to join us and said, "My dad's gonna build a new barn in the spring."

9

DAYS OF LIGHT AND SHADOW

DAYS OF CHILDHOOD ARE OFTEN REMEMBERED AS DAYS of either light or shadow. Those days when a bubbling sense of happiness came to stay in my heart seem to be associated with sunshine and golden light streamers that creased in through the green of my window-shade in the morning and stayed with me all day. Days of unhappiness are associated with the grey days of mid-winter when the wind played icy fingers on my backbone and the sky glowered at me with the face of a dark bully.

It is strange how some days could start with a sense of happiness that even subsequent trouble couldn't diminish. I heard Father singing in a hearty off-key as he started the fire in the kitchen stove. Lying in bed I could imagine the smell of the oven-dried cedar as he placed it on the torn-up paper after trying to coax life into the coals.

I knew the fire had started when that rushing sound came like wind in a tunnel through the pipe that meandered through my bedroom to the chimney. Then came the "tick-tick" of the igniting soot and the expansion of the stove-pipes, signalling that in a few minutes I could creep to the lee of the warming pipe as I dressed.

On the bright days I peeked into Grandfather's room. The eyes would twinkle in the age-reddened and wrinkled face.

"Guess I won't get up to-day," he would say, reaching for the pipe and matches on the table. "Don't tell your Ma I'm smoking in bed."

I didn't have to tell Mother: she knew as soon as the acrid fumes of the strong tobacco seeped into the hallway and wraiths of its blue smoke floated on the icy air of the unheated space outside her bedroom door.

This was the morning when the fire caught and the kitchen was warm. The porridge sitting in the double boiler on the back of the stove tasted so much better than it sometimes did and Mother pretended not to notice the size of the helping of brown sugar.

This was the morning when the brindle cow didn't kick the pail. It was a time when the Guernsey didn't swipe my face with her manure-laden tail.

There was fun in thawing out the pump and watching the crystal, gurgling water spill out into the barnyard trough as the stock clustered around, breaking through the frost-hardened crust of earth saturated by daily watering.

Those were the days when I was lucky enough to hitch a ride with Sandy Carter on his sleigh as he went to feed his cattle on the "other place." By the time we got to the school he would have a whole load of giggling children. Sandy was a tease and the girls would redden as he enquired about various juvenile "affairs of the heart."

If it were a good day the teacher had had a letter from home or a pleasant evening with a young man, or something to make her voice sound like "elfin bells." And so the day went, with no embarrassing moments of mental blankness in front of the blackboard or the class. It ended with the comfort of sitting at home with the ticking of the clock, the creaking of Grandfather's rocker and an unspoken feeling of harmony, until it was time for evening prayers and the trip to the feather bed mattress upstairs.

The unhappy days were associated with the times when the darkness of night seemed to merge into a grey day. It was like the perpetual twilight of the north. I heard Father grumbling as he slammed stove lids because the kindling wouldn't ignite. Grandpa barely opened his eyes when I looked in and I knew the misery of the aged was in his bones and that he would spend the day on the kitchen sofa.

It was a time of sharp words. All of us were so edgy that the squeak of a knife or fork on the plate seemed to cause electrical vibrations in our teeth.

The animals in the stable were balky. The brindle cow was obstinate and when I banged her on the flanks with the milking stool, Father was angry and red in the face as he shouted at me. The pump refused to be primed and I could feel the cold frost needling through my mittens as I pumped and pumped and wondered if the stock would ever get their fill of water.

Driving the stock back into the stable, I found that a cow had negotiated the fence gateway and was hightailing across a field of deep snow. I was hot and exhausted when I had finally driven her back into the stable, where she tried to crowd into the wrong stall. It was the morning I missed Sandy Carter. The narrow track of the freshly plowed roadway was difficult to walk in because I kept sliding into the deep snow. I was a quarter of a mile from the school when the bell started ringing. The teacher was grim and no explanations were accepted, so I was penalized a recess.

The sweat on my body seemed to congeal to ice and, try as I might, the lessons I had learned the night before wouldn't come to mind. I wanted to scream at the sound of chalk on the blackboard and the squealing of pencils on the slates of the primer class.

Supper was a quiet affair. I knew it had been one of those days at home, too; that Grandfather had kept silent and Mother and Father had built little animosities into a frozen war. It was a time when I waited until Father had mumbled evening prayers in a taut, quiet voice, before streaking for the security of the feather bed.

Then as I tried vainly to capture the phantom of sleep, I wondered about the difference between light- and shadow-days and hoped that by morning the sun would shine and Father would pinch Mother on the cheek before he left after breakfast to do the chores. I hoped that the twinkle would be back in the very old wise face of my grandfather, and that he would be released for awhile from the bondage of "the misery."

A strange restlessness seemed to come into the hearts of country people about the middle of winter. Perhaps this helped to explain the frequent occurrence of shadow-days not unrelieved, however, by the days of hope and light that heralded the approach of spring. The exuberance of frosty weather when skating and tobogganning were in full swing and the festivities of Christmas and the New Year had passed by. The youngsters felt a let-down after the school concerts and the spinsters relinquished hope when nothing happened after the Valentine Box Social.

Boys and girls faced the daily routine of going to school. Farmers grumbled a bit about the tedium of daily chores and found more and more excuses to go into town. The talk at the grist mill veered away from cutting wood or opening the vegetable pit to thoughts of getting the sugar shanty in shape. Each renewed storm or cold spell halted only temporarily the half-hearted attempt in the granary to clean seed.

At this season of the year, I noticed harsh replies at the breakfast table. There was a retort flung over a rigid shoulder. Father's mouth set in a firm line. Mother stood looking out the window and her foot was tapping. The tension developed during the day. Dinner was distinctly uncomfortable, so I bolted my food and left the house. A cap or a mackinaw left lying on a chair brought a sharp reprimand. Supper by lamplight was a silent affair and I had the same feeling that hovers in the air on a summer day before a storm.

The unproductive days of winter had begun to wear thin. The natural urge of the farmer who wants to start another growing season produced this tension. I have often wondered how it was that I instinctively knew that this had all faded away when I got up one morning. The winter birds that I hadn't noticed all winter were chattering away in the big tree beside the house. There was a bright sun shining, shattering into millions of splinters of reflected light on the crusted snow. Even this early in the morning, the icicles on the sunny side of the house had started to weep the lament of winter's passing.

The kitchen range was spluttering with warmth and the kettle was steaming. The old cat, content to snooze most of the time in cold weather beside the woodbox, stood waiting to get outside. Father was whistling as he brought in the fresh milk from the first milking for breakfast. I noticed that the cattle, instead of huddling in the lee of the strawstack in the well-worn-out spots, were milling about churning the snow and the softened mud into a sticky morass.

I once asked my mother how it was that she knew the right time to plant the seeds.

"It's easy. When your father starts snapping and acts as if he were itchy and doesn't know that we've reached the point where the weather is going to turn," she smiled.

Somehow winter was like climbing a hill. We laboured up one side and when the evening of a certain day came, we reached the summit in darkness. Then, when dawn broke the next morning, we started the descent on the other side toward spring.

Day by day the sun got stronger and stronger. The crusted snow started to "shell," and the pitch-holes increased on the concession. Where the springs welled up beside the creek in the Long Swamp there was an open patch of water. Invariably someone showed up at school who had ventured on thin ice and fallen in. The very smell of his steaming clothes beside the box stove gave reassurance to the hope that the awakening season was approaching.

On soft days I heard a multitude of sounds. The old freight-train groaned with exertion on the grade out of the valley. Blue jays scolded us in the woods as we cleaned out the sugar shanty, unearthing a stock of beechnuts cached by a squirrel. That worthy creature chattered profanely as we desecrated his food tomb.

There were things about the house that I noticed. The linoleum seemed to sparkle where the sun hit it. The nickel on the range refracted the sunshine. Some of the house plants were blooming profusely and I watched for the little green shoots from the egg cups, tins and five-pound cheese boxes on the window sill.

We were still in for more snow and some freezing cold, but it didn't seem to bother a farmer. The fanning mill was going in the granary as the seed was cleaned. The first day that had a certain warmth in the sun the trees were tapped in the sugar bush. By day I saw the steam clouds pouring up into the crisp air and by night the ceremonial fires were tended.

It would have been hard to dampen the enthusiasm of the man who was on his way downhill to the warm spring valley of growing things and the season of spring.

SPRING

10

EASTER AND SPRING PROMISE

I HAVE ALWAYS FELT THAT ONE SPECIAL EASTER DURING the Depression taught me the true meaning of charity and tolerance. It seemed that the latent spirit, once made free from self-pity, rolled on in boundless waves.

During a Depression winter we had skating on the river and hard-time dances in the township hall, arranged so that people whose clothes were old and patched would not be ashamed to come. Pigs sold at three dollars a hundredweight and cream and eggs were practically worthless. It always made us angry to read in the city papers that all the produce was still selling at comparatively high prices. In spite of the hard times, though, we had fuel for the fire and food to eat, even if there was hardly any cash in the old sideboard bureau or the cracked teapot.

The schoolteacher hadn't been paid in months and started spending a month apiece at different homes. The tax collector was idle most of the time. Doctor Macdonald said he began to feel like the owner of a packing plant because of the number of sides of pork or beef tendered in lieu of his charges for delivering babies. Going to buy some staples such as tea and sugar, a man felt he had to take something to Tim Murphy and the usual tender was a load of wood. This had to stop, however, when the backyard of Murphy's store began to look like a monster woodlot. I remember once finding a penny on the road and spending a delicious hour hovering over the candy case trying to decide whether to take two bull's-eye candies or two licorice pipes. Finally the clerk suggested one bull's-eye and one licorice pipe.

Toward the end of that third winter a melancholia seemed to settle over people on our concession. The teacher threatened to get married to a man who worked for the county on the roads. The butcher at the beef ring wanted to get some money in place of having always to take meat. With no hope of a price increase, and most granaries well stocked with the crop of the season before, farmers hesitated about the seeding. Easter was coming up and most people dreaded the ordeal of putting on brave faces for the season that was supposed to represent hope and joy. Three days before Easter, Tim Murphy put a sign up, saying that he could no longer extend credit or barter because the wholesalers would not give him goods without cash.

In our house there was a winter bitterness. When we heard that Bert Davidson was moving from the city to live on the old Barton place, it gave us a certain bitter satisfaction. Bert was the boy who had hit the high spots on the inheritance left by his father. When he married Alice Kennedy, a girl thought to be snooty because of a college education, it brought the old fires of prejudice to a full flame. Bert was Protestant and Alice was Catholic. We had heard stories about their big home in the city and of how Bert was making a fortune in stocks and bonds. Once he had come back driving a foreign sports car, throwing up dust on the main street and smoking fancy cigars.

We heard that the Barton place, which had been deserted for years, was all that was left of the Davidson legacy, and that Bert had gone broke. On the Thursday before Easter a car drove into our lane. It was the Model T owned by Father

Donovan and to our amazement he had Reverend McPherson of the Methodist Church with him. They explained simply that they wanted help in cleaning up the old Barton house because the Davidsons were arriving on Saturday with their four children.

Maybe it was the sight of the clergymen together that started us all off; maybe we just needed a spur to help us forget our own troubles. Anyway, by afternoon the Barton place was swarming with people. They found window-glass to replace the panes broken by wandering boys. The roof was patched and the lean taken out of the veranda. There was a sugar kettle of water boiling in the orchard and the women were scrubbing and polishing inside. Ed Higgins, the fellow who had been the loudest in his condemnation of Davidson, appeared with a cook stove which he said had been rusting in his woodshed. Extra chairs and tables appeared and clean, if somewhat garish, wall paper was applied in the living-room.

The sight of the priest and the minister in their shirt sleeves, burning brush and obviously enjoying it, was a satisfaction in itself. With the magic that all women have, food appeared along with gallons of scalding tea. People of the community who had barely spoken to each other were chatting and talking in the most friendly way. The road gate was fixed and painted and the well was cleaned. When everything was finished on the Saturday morning before Easter, people lingered to admire their handiwork.

That's when Tim Murphy's half-ton truck drove up with Mrs. Davidson sitting in the cab holding her baby, and the others in the back. It was a far cry from a sports car. There was a silence when they came up. Bert Davidson climbed down from the truck and just stood there. I can still see the lines on his face and the streak of premature grey hair under his hat. No one said anything until Alice, the tears streaming down her face, exclaimed, "Thank God," and then, with a humility that none of us had ever seen in him before, Bert Davidson took off his hat and said, "But we have nothing to give you in return." That's when Father Donovan said, "But you have, Bert. You have faith in your neighbours." The Reverend McPherson nodded and said, "And you have love for your neighbours."

Everybody felt it, but country people become a little embarrassed by statements like that so we drifted off while the

Davidsons stood there looking a little dazed. Knots of people stood on the road or around buggies and cars and there was a general air of something like optimism. Instead of thinking about our own troubles we were planning how we could help Alice and Bert Davidson, the old resentment about spendthrift ways and religion having somehow vanished like the dust and dirt of the house before the determined women.

Next day was Easter Sunday and there was a full turn-out. Both the Methodist Church and the Catholic Church were packed. There wasn't much new finery. There may have been an odd coat or suit that had been dyed or a few hats that had been given a feather or two. In spite of the hard times there was a kind of shiny hopefulness about all the people that Easter Sunday morning. It was the kind of bright look that can only come when souls have been scrubbed.

We called it a town, but it was really only a village. Just the same it held many delights for a small farm boy. This was especially true on a spring afternoon when I was allowed to go "in" with Father to take a load of grist to the mill.

There was a greenish tint over the brown waste on the fields and hills. Fall seeding was showing up like green whiskers on the dark earth. The pussy willows had popped their "kittens" on slender stems that hung over the creek, swollen by melting ice and run-off water. Cattle stood around in barnyards while a few dogs nosed on sandy hillsides, anticipating groundhogs. Other dogs came yapping down laneways as if they couldn't contain their spirits on such a bright day. Here and there, a late maple syrup shanty sent stray rings and spirals of smoke filtering up through the trees to vanish into the void of blue sky and occasional cloud.

Spring was a special time on the farm. Even as I noticed that things were different on the way to town, so I scooped up each day of warming enjoyment around the farm. One of the joys for a youngster came in the abundance of water.

Now, every boy has a penchant for water. It doesn't matter if he is the offspring of landlubbers or not. Some instinct prompts a lad to be a paddler and a dabbler as soon as the warming sun sends the melted snow to clutch at the ice bonds of the creeks and rivers. The streams swell up with ice, some of which melts, the rest sweeping downstream in a swollen mass to tear at river banks and threaten bridges and dams.

Normally respectable, meandering streams that barely wet sand and gravel bottoms during a natural summer become raging, roaring torrents in the spring. The unleashed power, both fearful and fascinating, acts as a magnet for every small boy. From time to time some boy of the township yielded to its siren call and fell in while trying to navigate one of the spring-maddened waters.

All puddles were made for dabbing at with sticks. A country boy who was not equipped with knee-high rubber boots was considered to be underprivileged. Even with this armour, I managed at least once or twice to get in over the top of my boots. There was a delicious sense of daring in edging at rotten, bank ice along the creek, only to lose footing and have a bootful of icy water slop in. I either dumped the water on the spot and wrung out the sock, or else I squelched on to school. I was secure in the knowledge that I had a reasonable alibi—"I slipped"—which a teacher could hardly believe. On the other hand, she was certainly not going to risk my getting a cold from having wet socks, so an entire morning, or most of it, was idled away while I toasted my feet and socks beside the box stove.

Every spring the Maitland River, a crooked stream that slithered in as long a route as possible towards Lake Huron, suddenly came to life and became a raging torrent. I woke one night with the spatter of soft, spring rain on the windows and the roof to hear a dull roar in the distance. There was an electric quality in the knowledge that the ice was breaking up. Somehow or other I had to manage a trip to town.

Just to approach the bridge and see the great chunks of ice, bearing burdens of debris of all kinds! The creeping earthworm of a river had become a mighty, coiling, raging python. Whole trees, and man's discard from old stoves to dead cows, were borne along easily on the bosom of the river. Always there were the grinding, tearing and smashing chunks of ice, tearing at soft banks and ripping out small trees, carrying a great mass protest to be slapped up against the bridge foundations or the mill dam. It seemed as if the river wanted to bulwark against its own strength and then flood out across the country.

The spring floods brought dreams of adventure. We could dream of building a raft and taking provisions and floating down the river and out to sea. These were personal dreams because if I dropped a hint of them I received from Mother dire warnings and from Father an amused tolerance.

Time and the sun wore away the defiance of the rivers and streams. The ice melted, the raging river subsided and the world took on a new green from field to tree. By night the frogs chorused in the wet swamp and the crows scolded by day. Sea gulls swooped and pirouetted, following the plows as they unearthed unwary worms and delicious grubs for their probing beaks.

There was a promise in the air. In my heart there was a kind of exuberance that made me want to run and gambol like the new colt. Even school could be tolerated for a while because I knew that time would pass and the freedom of summer holidays would come and give me two months' leave of the kind of work that palled so terribly when the world was warm again.

11

PURGES AND LUMBERJACKS

BY WHAT DIVINE RITE WAS IT THAT EVERY SPRING when I was a child in the country I became the victim of the so-called "spring tonic"? I was led to believe that during the dreary, dark days of the winter season my blood, in some mysterious fashion, had accumulated poisons of all kinds. These simply had to be purged out when the new season came along.

This rite was a hangover from pagan days. I think it must have had something to do with sacrifice. Probably the pagans lined all their children up and gave each of them a draught on the first day when the sun shone warmly. Every seventh or tenth one was given poison hemlock instead and this was their way of offering a sacrifice to the gods for having come through the winter with only a few minor cases of malnutrition or scurvy.

First of all, there was among these purges the dreaded senna leaf. If I gave a sign of a cough or a cold or even a sniffle which was probably only an allergy, I was given the Senna Tea Rite. This was a foul concoction boiled on the stove. (Sometimes the leaves were only steeped in hot water.) The dreadful brew was drained off and I was administered a portion. Girls were allowed to put cream and sugar in it. It wasn't manly for a boy to take it any way but straight. This was what they called a stomach settler.

Of course, that was only part of the treatment. Before going to bed I was given a copious quantity of Epsom salts which was guaranteed to unsettle my stomach all over again.

I was once caught in a dreadful situation. Having had my purge I went to visit with some cousins on the fourth concession. My aunt was a formidable woman with ten children, a quiet husband and a will of iron. It was my misfortune to arrive on Burdock Day. My aunt had unquenchable faith in the mystical powers of burdock to promote health of all kinds.

The burdock may not appear to be much to a passerby in the country, seeing it grow in profusion. To my aunt it was put there by God for the divine purpose of helping her in all her misfortunes, including her brood. She used it for poultices and for purifying maple syrup, having jars of burdock extract always on hand. Burdock leaves inside a bandage wrapped around your head would banish headaches. If she had been a religious woman I believe she would have used it for the purpose of saving souls.

On this particular occasion I arrived just when the first tender burdocks were out. I smelled something strange in the kitchen in midafternoon but in the helter-skelter of playing I forgot about it. I noticed her gathering something from around the driving-shed and asked one of my cousins about it. He just grinned and said, "You'll find out." He was never very fond of me anyhow.

When we came in for supper at the sound of the clanging on the old angle-iron I noticed a certain reluctance on the part of the family. Uncle was stern and my aunt, a woman of great size and strength, appeared with a willow switch. There was an air around the supper table of innocents going to the slaughter. Just the same there was a splendid aroma inside that kitchen. Everyone lined up and my uncle said grace. We sat down and I reached for some bread and then noticed that no one was passing anything. Usually in that home they started like a threshing gang.

Then I noticed the glass. It was almost full and it was a sickening colour that was neither green nor brown. My aunt picked hers up and said, "Well, you certainly are in luck tonight, Harry. This is really our spring cleaning night. Here's to all our healths."

There was a decided lack of enthusiasm for spring cleaning. My uncle slid a tentative hand towards his and pulled it a couple of inches nearer. I said, "What is it, Auntie?" She smiled the smile of the conqueror. "It's burdock tonic, made from fresh young burdock and it's probably the healthiest thing you'll ever get in your life."

Triumphantly my aunt downed her glass. I was hungry so I picked up my glass just as I saw my uncle wince and gasp over his. It was too late, however, because I had already opened up and the fatal liquid was dribbling into my mouth. Horror of horrors! Senna leaves tasted like candy in comparison with this stuff. I gagged and coughed and thought I was going to be sick, but burdock tonic has a great staying power. I watched my ten cousins in unison close their eyes and swallow the potion.

The unfortunate part of it was that everything I ate for supper tasted like burdock.

Fortunately, the spring season also had its compensations.

When I was a small boy in the country there was a tradition that the men-folk, at least those who could get away, went to work in the lumber woods during the winter. A mother and the older children would look after the chores while the father went to make some cash. In some cases an elder son would go away in October or early November and return in time to help with seeding.

One day in the spring when the wind whispered soft and the knolls were dry and only the hollows in the plowed fields looked dark and moist, I suddenly sensed that the lumberjacks would be coming back. Within a day or two Uncle Jack would come strolling down the road from the village, a pack on his back, wearing a bright mackinaw and a knitted cap and clenching a pipe between his teeth. He would also be sporting magnificent bright sandy whiskers.

Uncle Jack was my hero. He had already gone to the bush for three years and he was only twenty-one or twenty-two.

Every time he had been away he brought me back something.

My mother always irritated me when Jack returned. She ran halfway down to the road gate and cried a little and then laughed a little and then cried a little more. Beside the hulking six-foot-two giant with the pack and the massive coat she looked like a midget. He laughed and picked her up off her feet and swung her around, saying, "Well, old girl, the wolves didn't eat me this time but they came mighty close."

Later, in the house, I crouched as close as I could to him while my mother fed him tea and cake. Cake was the one thing he wanted and a cake didn't last long.

"You see, we got all the meat and potatoes and pie we could eat," Jack laughed between slabs of cake.

It was from him that I learned at first hand about the hiring in Bay City or Saginaw. The agents of the lumber companies set up in a saloon or a hotel lobby and hired men. Sometimes when the recruiting was slow they were not above a bit of bribery in the form of free whiskey. A lumberjack occasionally found himself waking up on a sleigh bound for the remote camps.

It was easy to picture the loaded sleighs setting out with supplies and men, heading through the snowy back roads that drifted in after them, to be broken only once every fortnight when a supply team brought in mail and extra supplies. Sometimes in the dead of winter when the snow had piled high, the supply teams couldn't make it for six weeks at a time, and the men were truly snow-locked in the bush.

As Jack talked it was easy to imagine the low, timbered shanties. There were the bunkhouses where the men slept, the cook shanty adjoining the mess hall and the long, log stables where the horses were kept. I was fascinated by the description of the bunkhouses. Sixty men would be quartered in this place, heated by two enormous box stoves. Overhead there was constantly hanging an assortment of laundered socks and undershirts. Around the table was a perpetual card game and a checker game, but without gambling. The foreman was strict about this.

Some men talked, while some turned in after supper and stayed there until the five o'clock call in the morning. I could imagine the scene when the lanterns were turned low and the men were all in their bunks and the symphony of snores started. I could also sense the feel of the frost at five in the morning or hear, in the middle of the night when the northern lights crackled with breathless static, the sound of timber wolves.

Jack was one of my first heroes. Somewhere in a trunk I still have the team of horses he whittled out during long nights in the bunkhouse and brought back as a gift.

On the Sunday following the return of the lumberjacks, there were always at least ten beards at church. The younger girls had no eyes for the married ones. They clustered around the bachelors, like Jack and, as I remember, at my tender age I was extremely jealous of them. I wondered what he could see in talking to silly girls.

Meanwhile, with my newly acquired knowledge I was able to speak knowingly at school about the log drive and a jam-up. It was easy to sprinkle conversation with such words as cant-hook and peavy and I had myself almost convinced that I could birl a log. On a cold day in early May an experiment I conducted with a log in the river almost ended in catastrophe. In fact, in the turbulent spring waters of the river, I would have been drowned if the mailman hadn't stopped to drop an enquiring fishline over the bridge. My birling ended ignominiously at the end of a branch which he extended as a lifeline from the bank.

As for the beards, they survived two or three appearances at church and at the Friday-night dances in the township hall. Then the weather turned warmer, the seeding started, and somehow they seemed to vanish.

That was the cue for my mother to sigh and say, "Thank heavens Jack has taken that fur off. It may be all right in a lumber camp but it looks sort of scratchy here."

12
HAPPY TIMES

FROM THE TIME THE FIRST FURROWS WERE creased across our fields until the corn was planted, our farm had an air of bustle about it. I could sense the pulse of things growing. It seemed almost as if I could stop in the laneway and feel the surge of life-giving sap in grass and plants.

They were days of change. At first the trees were tinged a faint green and suddenly, as if overnight, they broke into full leaf. The air came in heavy and fertile with promise through open doors and windows.

The really definite sense of the change in seasons came when Father let the stock out to grass. The happy time may have been influenced by the relief I had in knowing that there would be much less work to do in the stables.

When the ground had dried enough that I could flop down

on it and have a snooze after dinner without danger of rheumatism flaring up, I knew that the season for leaving the cattle on the pasture overnight had come in earnest.

In the garden the Dutch setts sprang forth like green guards and the radishes peeked through and were bushing out. The front lawn had progressed from a bristle of grass to a full stand that had to be cut or exposed to the close-cropping sheep. The nights had lost their chill and it was most unusual if we got another bad frost.

The cattle seemed to know what was happening. That was one of the strange things about cattle. If we drove them out the front laneway on their way to market, they raised a ruckus. On the other hand, when we drove them out the laneway on their way to the grass farm on the concession they responded meekly.

When we got them to the grass it was a different matter. They set to cropping the grass furiously, as if it were the prelude to starvation. After a time they stopped and the younger ones began bunting and pushing. It was very like youngsters on their way home on the last day of school.

Cows were different. They approached a pasture field warily after a winter of being cooped up in a barn. Like a ladies' auxiliary of any organization, a herd of cows had one poke-and-snoop character. She was self-appointed to investigate every possible avenue of escape and adventure.

We had a brindle cow, called Jessie, with a crooked horn. I often felt that she must have had that horn twisted on purpose by the devil. Jessie could perform the most outlandish feats of escape. If her stanchion chains weren't just right she diligently worked at them with her horn. Once she was loose, it was easy for her to unhook the stable door. She was an artist when it came to opening gates.

During the first week that the cows were on pasture Jessie spent her time investigating. Someone kept her under watch during this time. If there was a post where the fence hung on weak staples she found it, and we immediately fixed it.

Try as we might to reinforce the fence around the drain that ran through our farm and the Higgins' place, she usually found some avenue of escape where the run-off water in the early spring had weakened a post, or ice had jarred the fencing loose. Sure enough, there was always a morning when Higgins called in the dawning hours and said, "Will you get that blasted cow out of my clover?"

Having proven to her satisfaction and the satisfaction of the other members of the herd that she could breach the line fence, she then concentrated on the straight rail fence between the pasture and the field where the corn and root crops were growing. Going down to the barn one morning we found her in the corn patch, filled to bursting with her night meal and grinning in an almost derisive way. Next she found the weak spot in the fence around the garden. She timed this perfectly with the ripening of the new lettuce and cabbages.

Horses were always a source of enjoyment during the happy times. On a Sunday I liked to steal a few lumps of sugar from the pantry when Mother was upstairs making the beds and then head for the pasture field. Old Belle, the matriarch mare, had an uncanny instinct for knowing when you were coming to give her a treat, as opposed to when you wanted to hitch her to the buggy or the democrat. In the latter case she would be back at the woods or in the swale. In the first case she would be waiting at the lane gateway.

Colts let out to pasture always acted like little clowns. The late Pete McArthur put it well when he said that he enjoyed watching colts either when they were snorting at their kick or kicking at their snort. There was a world of enjoyment for man and beast when the stock had been let out to pasture.

For some reason, in the spring and early summer days I did a lot of whistling. Everybody seemed to whistle then.

Whistling was an art that developed by degrees. While still in my tender years I used to marvel at the ability of one hired man to whistle in a way that was a delight. He was whistling all the time except when he was asleep, and even then my father maintained that he half whistled in place of snoring.

Grandfather was never much of a whistler. Lips puckered up over toothless gums, his whistling was generally limited to rustling the shaggy ends of his moustache. His performance was hampered by lack of a knowledge of tunes, although he was vain enough to feel that his rendition of "The Flowers of Edinburgh" was truly masterful. If someone suggested that he whistle at a family gathering, Grandmother always warned him not to, but he would push her aside with a playful little tap of his hand and proceed with a great deal of gusto to perform, much to the amusement of his guests.

Aunt Millie had a soft whistle. It was shrill at times, when it slipped off key—a frequent occurrence. As a matter of fact it was one of the most distracting whistles I have ever heard. Even a tone-deaf person could recognize that Millie was a sort of musical rag-picker, picking up odd phrases and keys and mixing them into a disturbing *mélange.*

Grandmother, who was musical by nature, put up with it for just so long.

"Millie, for the love of life and liberty!" Grandmother exclaimed. "Will you stop that noise? You sound like a bag of drowning kittens!"

Millie was hurt and retired to her bedroom to pout. After Grandmother had made a cup of tea to soothe her, Millie went back to work. Within a half hour the whistling mania came over her again, leading to another scene, and so on all day.

People used to be conceited about their whistling. It was considered a credit to the family to have a good whistler in it. They were in constant demand at garden parties and various social functions. The greatest misfortune that could befall a whistler was to be placed on an unsheltered platform on a windy night at a garden party or fowl supper. The notes would come out well enough, but the wind soon distorted them, and listening was something like tuning in shortwave on a night when the atmospherics are particularly bad.

Father was a whistler of no mean ability. He prided himself on being able at times to "double-whistle." To me it always seemed that he had an impediment of some kind but that didn't stop Father. Nevertheless there was something rather pleasant about the sound of the whistle. When the taxes were paid and things were going well we could hear him whistling on his way to and from the barn. At night in the stable by the flickering lantern light as he did the evening chores, the sound of that whistle always gave me a special feeling inside.

My first efforts in the direction of whistling took place in the barn or the barnyard when no one was around. Nevertheless I had some powerful critics. The hens cocked inquisitive eyes at me. The grey goose waddling across to the puddle beside the horse trough abandoned her plans and went back down the laneway to the pond. The barn cats fled to the house and the bull snorted, rattling his chains as if being pursued by a demon.

As a boy, I remained rather shy about whistling in public. I enjoyed it, but didn't have much confidence in the product. Therefore whistling was mainly done on the way to get the cows or drive them back to the pasture after milking. Being alone on the way to school also afforded an opportunity for some practice.

"My Wild Irish Rose" seemed to be the only tune I could manage but even it used to get caught up sometimes with overtones of a Gaelic ballad that Father tried to conquer. Daydreaming in school one day I was pursing my lips trying to get in a little, silent lip exercise, when by some strange mischance a whistle darted out. The teacher we had at that time was a harridan who didn't like boys and hated whistling. In a truly sadistic fashion she made me go up to the front of the room and whistle. Try as I might nothing would come out but a series of rude noises. This infuriated her and I took ten wallops on each hand from the hame strap she kept in her desk.

God, in His wondrous way, however, managed to punish that teacher. She became enamoured of a passing stranger and married him. It turned out later that he was a professional entertainer from a Chatauqua unit. He was a whistler.

13
FIRST MEMORIES

THE YARD WAS MY HOME WHEN I WAS VERY small. It figures in all of my first memories. The capital of this world was the fat, old log house with its clapboard sidings of knotted and weather-beaten wood.

In the world of the yard surrounding our house on the farm I can remember the orchard and the lawn that sloped down towards the lane fence and its row of poplars. They were green sentinels, always on guard, looking like tapers against the sky. There was the garden enclosure where my mother worked her magic from early spring until late fall. One fence ran along the dusty roadway, another edged the pasture field, one separated us from the world of the barnyard and the fourth intersected a small clump of willows, making a swampy world for exploration, especially in the spring before the hot summer sun dried up the water.

The fenced yard had places of mystery. There were refuges, such as the space under the front veranda or the patch of burdocks in the corner. The ground was hard-packed and cool and I could peer out and wait until my mother came to look absent-mindedly out of the back door. She would turn away and then, remembering, call out in alarm. If I timed it perfectly she would have come to the veranda before I ventured out of the hiding-place. In her relief she often provided a ransom of cookies and cool milk from the pan in the old stone milk-house.

It was largely a world of play. There was a sand-pile behind the back kitchen, left after a new ceiling had been put up in the parlour. Broken shingles, bits of harness leather, empty spools, exploded cartridge cases from the rifle club—all these were the tools of play. There was no thought of store toys. The occasional one that happened to be forwarded by a city relative was treasured for special occasions. Imagination and the items discarded from a man's world made up the toys during those days.

I had sand castles, muddy ditches that seemed like roaring streams, puddles stirred into facsimiles of raging seas, a hoop to roll, or a house made by draping old sacks from the side of a discarded democrat behind the driving-shed. A tattered saddle tacked on a saw-horse was a worthy steed.

It wasn't such a bad life. Barn cats could be induced to come and romp with their kittens when the grass grew tall under the apple trees. The blossoms came out on the fruit trees, the lilacs cast a cloud of scent around the front porch and the Dutchman's Pipe spread out broad, protecting leaves on the south side of the house. There was the mystery of the morning glories on the shady side of the house. They remained in full bloom until the first peeks of sun came across the end of the veranda. Mother's beds of zinnias, asters and marigolds spread colourful patterns in the two whitewashed binder wheels decorating the front lawn.

Thinking about it now, I often try to remember what the world of a child was really like. There was always the matter of being alone, but somehow remembrance doesn't carry with it thoughts of loneliness. I can remember my mother singing in the kitchen. Sometimes she scrubbed clothes in the old tub on the flat maple stump beside the pump stand. I can remember clothes flapping in the breeze on the line, reminding me of ships in full sail. Other times she churned milk, and the throaty, clunking gears of the barrel churn in the echoing milk-house sounded a bit like soft summer thunder in the distance. There seemed to be so many things to do in those pre-school days in the square world of a yard, although activities were always tied to the home base of the squat old house, with its front windows that looked like eyes peeking out roadwards all the time.

An ant-hill beside the driving-shed supplied a minor world of animation. The black specks in their organized confusion held me fascinated. When the interest was gone, cruelty brought on by boredom supplied the motive for a drowning incident with dipperfuls of water from the old tub where it was warming for the evening ritual of watering the garden. This sent the little fellows helter-skelter. A savage jab with a stick brought a catastrophe which they painstakingly repaired. But I wasn't interested in the repairs. Some other interest would come along then.

In the middle of the long childhood afternoons I was always excited to see a dust-cluster over the hill of our valley. Soon a horse and buggy slid down the face of the hill and vanished into the swale. By the time I had raced to the gateway, I heard the hollow rumble of the hooves and wheels on the creek bridge. It was Joe, the mailman, and he waved at first sight.

The horse and buggy swooped into the gateway. Joe was badly crippled and sat hunched in one side of the sagging buggy. He always said, "No mail," and then cackling with laughter at my woe-begone look, flourished a newspaper which he tossed across the gate. Letters, and the abundance of advertising which now flood the mails, were practically non-existent in those days. Red-letter days in mail collecting were marked by the arrival of Eaton's and Simpson's mail order catalogues for fall and winter or spring and summer. Grandfather's annual mail was the fur catalogue of prices from Hallam's because he kept his hand in at trapping for muskrats and occasionally foxes.

I puzzled over the *Globe* as I trudged up the laneway. There weren't many pictures and I couldn't read. By the time I arrived at the house Mother was pouring herself a cup of tea. Sometimes she answered my questions about some strange thing in the paper but usually she seemed lost in another world as she read.

Quite often my father found a reason for visiting the house. Soon he was drinking tea and looking over a portion of the paper. Try as I might, the lure of the old sofa in the kitchen overcame me and without any effort I drifted off to sleep. There was always a hazy flurry of calendar on the wall, the magazine rack, the old clock on the sideboard shelf and the throaty gurgling of the tea-kettle with the small, protesting squeak of the boards under the rocking chairs that helped to lull me away. I didn't want to go to sleep but I didn't mind, either.

There was another world outside the yard fence that was barred to me, unless I was in the company of my father, mother or grandfather.

I can vaguely remember peeking through the great planked X of the barnyard gate. The barn appeared big, too large for its mottled stone foundation. The rust-streaked tin roof seemed to have been jammed on as an afterthought, its narrow eaves making the whole thing look like a felt hat with trimmed brims. Swallows flitted through the air, swooping and darting in quick patterns while lazy, fat pigeons burbled all afternoon in their over-stuffed chests on the beams high over the mows of dusty, musky hay.

The barnyard, a wallow of mud in the spring and late fall, was dominated by a mushroom strawstack in summer and a steadily growing manure pile in winter. I knew that the barnyard held dangers. They ranged from the fiercely possessive Tamworth sow who lived in the mashy, smelling pigpen with her perpetual litter of piglets, to the oval water trough by the windmill. Dimly, I was aware that a cousin of mine had once vanished into the murky water of that trough. "Drowning" as a word had no meaning for me, so the danger was translated in terms of vanishing.

In the world across the gate I also had an enemy. He was a huge greenish-black rooster with a startling white collar and a plumage of orange and yellow tail feathers. Ethiopia strutted all day and preened himself, mocking the harem of hens by gobbling the advertised morsel of food after they had arrived at his call. The stamping and chain-rattling of the bull in the box stall ran a poor second in the way of danger in comparison with this fierce rooster.

Mother waged a physical and vocal war against Ethiopia, and never crossed the barnyard without a stout stick. She was not above taking a slice of air at him without direct cause. Father, on the other hand, respected the rooster and the latter respected Father's heavy boots with the steel-plated toes. Mother accused Father of secretly admiring the rooster for his propensity for scrapping.

Rip, a brown and white collie, was my envy in those days. While I was confined to the house yard, the dog was free to roam at will. His only duties were to bring up the cows morning and evening for milking and nip at the heels of any stray beast that might force the fence into Mother's garden. At other times he snoozed on the porch, chased groundhogs on the sandy hill in the pasture, yapped at passing vehicles or argued with stray dogs. Once or twice he came home in smelly disgrace after an encounter with a better-armed opponent, a skunk.

Ethiopia was the one fly in the contented ointment of Rip's existence. Somehow or other Rip could intimidate most of the other animals. Though maintaining a shaky armed truce with Sir Bernard, the bull, he could never reach an understanding with the arrogant rooster. More than once he sacrificed a strip of hide and hair to the sharp claws of his enemy. Rip would stay in the shade of the driving-shed with his nose nuzzled in his paws, apparently asleep but in reality watching Ethiopia. When family matters demanded Ethiopia's attention, the dog would explode into a noisy offensive. Ethiopia was never defeated in battle but he lost a few tail feathers which only heightened his appearance of arrogant insolence.

One day the inevitable happened: I walked through the barnyard gate, straight into the path of Ethiopia. The gate stood unlatched so I ventured into the yard, forgetting the ferocious rooster. I can still see Ethiopia going around me in diminishing circles while I stood in sheer terror and watched him closing in.

Something prompted me to run but a large clod of clay tripped me and I went down. Death seemed to be imminent and the whole thing is confused, although I dimly remember something scratching at my face. Rip was barking and I screamed when I felt the whiskers of Mr. Moses, the hired hand, on my cheek. I must have thought they were feathers.

Mr. Moses was saying, "Cool down, lad, but be sure and tell your father that the old rooster was scratching you. He was fond of that old pelter."

Ethiopia was dead. Mother was pleased, Grandfather chuckled and Mr. Moses wisely refrained from any comment as he explained how he demolished the feathered tyrant with a pitchfork.

The old rooster was replaced by a large, fat and amiable Barred Rock. Father maintained he was too fat to be any good. I didn't care because when the stock were not in the yard I could wander into the barnyard after that, if I remembered to stay carefully away from the water trough with its menace of making me vanish like my cousin.

14

THE HIRED MAN

THE HIRED MAN WAS AN INDISPENSABLE member of our farm life. Mr. Moses, a diminutive, wiry man who lived in a little house at the crossroads with his merry wife, was a seasonal worker for us. He came to help out when my grandfather was busy trapping, visiting with another relative or during one of the occasional periods when he retired to his own house as if wanting to enclose himself in complete privacy.

Hiring a man used to be an easy and casual affair. In town on Saturday night you either spotted a man looking for work or he came up and asked if you needed a "hand." He was hired for the following Monday. Sure enough, about daybreak on the following Monday he came down the road from the village carrying a battered valise or suitcase, or shouldering a knapsack. He was always given the eye by the women-folk in an attempt to determine whether he was clean or not.

The new hired man was generally installed in the bedroom over the kitchen. This semi-isolation was supposed to be a precaution against the unsanitary one that occasionally came along. Sometimes, in rush seasons like haying or harvesting, we even hired strangers from the road, who were installed, upon the insistence of the women, in the harness room of the driving-shed (at considerable risk, because of the number of them who smoked "makings" continuously).

A hired man soon got into the swing of things around the farm. He was usually a quiet fellow with a certain resignation to his fate as a labourer. If he was a good type he found time to light the fire in the kitchen stove in the morning, or saw that the woodbox was kept filled. In return the women saw that his darning and mending were attended to without any fuss.

Hours used to mean very little to hired men. They were usually the first up in the morning. In rush seasons meals were often hurried affairs, and the hired man finished eating, picked up his hat and left the kitchen first. This was according to some unwritten law that the few minutes after a meal might be needed by a farmer and his wife to air some private domestic problem.

Some hired men liked horses and others didn't. Those who had no liking for them naturally fell into the routine of bringing up the cows while I watered and stabled the horses. Chore-time was also accepted as another part of a hired man's duties. After supper the average hired man sat and smoked, occasionally looked at a newspaper, but more often than not just sat out on the back stoop and listened to the night.

They were a lonely breed in many ways. Local gossip had little interest for them and the world of news seemed alien. It was as if they lived in a world of their own.

I always remember the one we called Uncle Gus. A former lumberjack, born in Sweden, he was a methodical and patient worker. Other men could tear into a hayfield but Uncle Gus just plodded along, accomplishing as much by the end of the day as anybody else.

He wore bright red flannel shirts and a vest in which to carry his pipe and matches and tobacco. In summer-time he wore hob-nailed boots that drove the women to distraction, because of what they did to floors and linoleum. He stayed at home every night except Saturday. On that night he put on a fine shirt without a collar, greased his hair and went to the village. He purchased his needs and then sat with the others at the blacksmith shop until we were ready to go home. When war broke out he went back to Sweden. We never heard of him after that but we often wonder where he is now.

Oswald was a character we hired late one spring. He was a slow but steady talker and he moved with monotonous regularity from one story to the other, so that you never really knew the ending of any of them. He was the one who carried cleanliness to almost ridiculous lengths. Twice a week he washed his feet. In the winter-time he soaked them in a pan behind the kitchen stove. In the summer-time he moved out to the back stoop where he could smoke, soak and talk at the same time.

No matter who was visiting, Oswald carried out his ablutions in just the same way. In fact, it grew to be quite a joke in the neighbourhood. If people were coming over for an evening of talk and a game of euchre they were apt to call and inquire if that were Oswald's bathing evening. The strange part of it is that Oswald, a canny saver, bought his own farm and married the sloppiest housekeeper in the township.

We had another hired man by the name of Peter the Great. I don't know who pinned that on him because poor Peter had only one ambition in life and that was never to leave anything in the way of food on the table after a meal. He thought nothin of finishing his dessert and and then scooping the last of the potatoes, meat and gravy onto his plate and starting all over again. He was a renowned trencherman and people used to say he could go through three sittings at a threshing table.

Peter reckoned people on their table. The Hawkins were good people because Mrs. Hawkins made the best pumpkin pie in the township. He didn't like the Jenkins' place because Mrs. Jenkins couldn't boil water without burning it.

Some of our hired men were talkative and some were quiet. Some were clean and others weren't too particular. Some were light sleepers and others ripped and buzzed like sawing machines all night long.

Little Jimmy was a small but mighty worker. He slept hard, just as he worked. It was a ritual with him to have a sleep after his noon meal. He could flop down on the veranda, in a wagon box or over a chop bin and go sound asleep for ten minutes, and then be up and off as fresh as the first daisy in a pasture.

Some of the hired men turned in and washed the dishes and teased the hired girl. Others were shy, and one poor fellow blushed if you mentioned a cow having a calf.

Eddy, better known as Caruso, was the best hired man we ever had. He vanished every Saturday night into the village, and came down the concession early Sunday morning singing with the firmest of alcoholic inspiration.

It was haying time when Jeff arrived at our place. The days were long and hot and the air resounded with the clack of mowers and men shouting to horses. The nights were dewy and soft, haunted by strange late-summer sounds. It was the kind of evening I welcomed most, when Father and Grandfather sat on the back veranda smoking.

There was little conversation. They were weary from working in the sun. Their pipes glowed like little red coals in the gathering dusk.

From the pasture behind the driving-shed came the sounds of animals still cropping. From time to time a bat whirled from under the house eaves and whooshed mysteriously around. A shrill tree toad prayed for hot weather.

We could hear a man whistling as he came down the road. It was as if the whole night and the valley stopped to listen because the air was soundless when he stopped whistling. Then he started again and we knew he had turned in at the road gateway.

"Good evening," my father called out, when the fellow was a few feet from the veranda.

"Good evening, sir," came the voice from the gathering darkness. "The man at the store said you might need a hand for haying."

"Could be. Hungry?"

There was a pleasant chuckle as the man swung his pack down to the steps of the veranda.

"Been a long time since morning."

"Better come in and we'll get you something to eat."

"Thank you. My name's Jeff. Could I freshen up a bit?"

"Sure, the lad will give you the basin out at the back step."

That's how Jeff came to work at our place in that bitter summer when the Depression hit so hard. I can still see him sitting at the kitchen table. His face was tanned and lean and his hair stood up in front like a shock of wheat that has weathered in the field. His eyes were clear blue with wrinkles around them that looked sort of sad. His shirt was faded but clean. When it was time to go to bed, Mother told Father to put him in the bedroom over the kitchen. Most transients went to a cot in a small room in the driving-shed. This man was different.

I often think of the debt I owe Jeff. He spoke very little about himself, and during those hard times, when men had troubles of all kinds, my folks didn't pry into his personal history. They cautioned me not to, as well. Once I heard Mother say to my father, "Have you ever noticed the wedding ring on his little finger? There's a man who has had his share of trouble."

My father nodded.

"There's a pain in his eyes every time he watches a child."

One day Jeff came upon the old guitar hanging up in the driving-shed. Carefully he tightened the strings and then strummed it and asked me if anybody played it. I explained that my uncle had once taken a sudden desire to be popular and had bought the guitar from a mail order house. After three lessons he had decided his work-calloused fingers were too clumsy for the instrument and gave it up.

In our pre-radio days Jeff and the guitar became a source of wonderful entertainment. He sat on the back veranda playing and singing before bedtime. Grandfather enjoyed cowboy ballads such as "Bury Me Not On The Lone Prairie." Father liked anything that was Irish and Mother enjoyed sad songs. I begged for the peppy ones like "Pop Goes The Weasel."

Jeff also shared my interest in the world of books. I became accustomed to going with him every Saturday night to the village library. On a Sunday afternoon while the rest of the family slept we would go into the orchard and read under the apple trees.

It was a summer when prices were bad. Farmers were short of money and they couldn't even sell their produce.

When the haying and harvesting were finished, my father told Jeff he couldn't pay him any wages but he could stay on for his board and tobacco. I was glad. The gloom that seemed to hang over our place during the Depression was somehow lifted when he picked up the guitar and sang at night.

Then one day a letter came for him. It was typewritten and

we all pretended to be busy as he read it. For a long time he sat and held it in his hand after he read it.

"I have to go," he said quietly. "My wife, you see, is in the San at Gravenhurst. They don't expect her to live much longer."

He stood up before he went to his room and I can still hear his voice as he said, "My daughter would have been the same age as the lad here, if she had lived. We were hard up and there wasn't enough to eat."

He went to his room and I was sent to bed to stare into the darkness and cry a little over the mysteries of life which I didn't understand. In the morning Father drove him to the village and I noticed that he handed Jeff the old guitar when they got into the buggy.

For a time neighbours used to ask where the "singin' man" had gone. My father would say, "He left a while ago." They often said, "Those wandering ones never stay long in a place."

My father didn't bother to answer them. He knew better about Jeff, our "singin' man."

I remember him as a small man with a wisp of beard that was red and a thatch of grey hair that stood up like stubble in the fall. He had a pipe, going or dead, almost constantly in his mouth. My father liked him because he was a steady and dependable worker and my grandfather objected only to his prowess as a checker player.

His name was Emmet Kelly and he was our hired man. I remember him because when he talked at night in the good, comforting light of the lamp, our kitchen took on a magical quality. Mother looked up from knitting or darning, Father continued staring at his paper although I knew he was listening, and Grandfather would forget to light his pipe, or keep his rocker going, as we were introduced to the fairy people of Emmet's native Ireland.

It was a fertile ground for cultivation because the Irish ties were strong in our family. Emmet, with the stubby pipe gripped between, or dangling from his teeth, would tell us about the "deenee shee" or fairy people. They were a strange lot, the hordes of them that seemed to be just beyond the circle of light.

I grew up with a great respect for them because Emmet was careful to point out their fairness in being good to good people and evil to the bad ones. He insisted that they should always be called the "deenee mathe," or "good people." If you did they were sure to keep bad times and misfortune away from you.

It seemed that every band of fairies had one shoemaker who was called the "leprechaun."

The sound of fairy music was the "colshee." Emmet was long on stories and short on schooling, so I didn't know how to spell it until long after when I found it in the Gaelic as "ceol-sidhe."

There were many nights, however, even before the advent of radio, when lying awake in an upstairs bedroom I was positive that the fairies were dancing and playing on the lawn under the apple trees. It was strange that they vanished before I could get up enough courage to peek out the window.

My grandfather was somewhat weak in history and relied on stories which I suppose had been handed down for years. It was rank heresy to him when Emmet related that St. Patrick had been born at Dumbarton, in Scotland. The argument raged for several days around the anniversary of the saint's death on March 17. Emmet was a master story-teller. He sat and told yarns by the hour and was a welcome visitor to the store or the grist mill or the noon rests at threshing bees.

He related how Pat Donnely, a publican, had a habit of walking in his sleep in his native village in Ireland, somewhere near Cork. He would get up and walk down the street to his tavern to see if the doors were closed, and then walk back and get into bed, without having any remembrance of walking at all.

It seemed that the village had hired a new constable from another town. The first one, a local boy, had to be replaced because he was constantly getting into fist fights with local people. The new one had no knowledge of Pat's habit of walking in his sleep.

Pat came to on one of his sleep-walks with a start, when he found the constable grasping his clothes.

"What the devil are ye doin', man?" demanded the constable.

Pat mustered his dignity.

"Now look here, I'll have you know that I'm a somnambulist."

The constable looked puzzled.

"I don't care if you're a soomnobolist or even a Methodist, you'll not be walkin' these streets in your night-shirt."

Emmet's favourite story concerned a cousin of his who once went to Glasgow. Looking for reasonable lodgings he was put in with a barber in a double room. The barber was completely bald and the cousin, somewhat jolly with drink, ribbed him unmercifully.

Leaving a call with the desk clerk for early the next morning, he went to bed and slept soundly. The barber was annoyed at the fun-poking and when the Irishman went to sleep, the barber shaved off his hair. The clerk called the cousin before dawn and that worthy crept out, feeling somewhat the worse for wear.

Passing a mirror he stopped and removed his hat because his head felt funny. When he saw the bald head he exclaimed, "That damned fool of a clerk has called the wrong man."

Emmet stayed with us even after the Depression had started, when it was impossible to pay him any real wages. He knew that times were tough but he was assured of a welcome at all times. One night he left without saying goodbye and we knew that he had wanted to make it easy for everyone. We missed him and heard later that he had died in an old people's home in Western Canada.

I often think of Emmet. I am certain that he must have made the twilight years more enjoyable for the other old folks in the home before he died.

Our hired men were all different, but all alike in a sense. Most of them treasured the hope of some day getting a place of their own, and yet most of them knew down in their hearts that unless some good fortune came along they would never be able to save enough money out of their small wages.

We had one feeling about all of them, after working and living with them for so long, and that concerned their leaving. We hated to see them come down the stairs with their old valises or knapsacks packed and watch them shift awkwardly and finally say, "I guess I better be gettin' along. I want to thank you . . . and the missus . . . for . . . for all the things you done for me."

As we watched them trudge down the concession, on the move again, we wondered in our hearts, at times, if maybe we couldn't have done something more for them.

15

DAYS OF GROWING UP

MY MOST VIVID MEMORIES OF GROWING FROM BOY to man seem to be of those changes in my outward appearance which didn't have much to do with preparing me for life in a grown-ups' world. But at the time, the kind of clothes I wore seemed to indicate with whom I should cast my lot, and I was anxious to be considered a man.

The problem of long pants versus short pants arose from a chance encounter with a cousin of mine from the tenth concession. Mother had salvaged the legs from the pants of a blue suit of my father. It was a shiny, blue serge, that had turned greenish with age and use. The cut-down seat and short legs were tailored into a pair of short pants for me.

They were new and I might even have been a bit proud of them. My problem was that I couldn't for the life of me see why I had to change from my overalls simply to go into town. When my father wore a clean pair of overalls I had to wear short pants.

While Father talked in the machine shop I strolled down the street.

"Hello there," came a greeting in a tone of voice that I could recognize anywhere.

It was my cousin Harold from the tenth concession. As far as I was concerned he was pure poison.

On this occasion I was at a disadvantage, because we met on Main Street, where there were no stones, clumps of dried manure or sticks to use as ammunition. Although we were the same age he was smaller than I was, which made the fact that he was wearing long pants of the bought kind more painful and embarrassing. He stared with contempt at my short home-made pants.

"Mother says I am a man now," he smirked, munching on candy.

I didn't mind his not offering me any candy. I was prepared for that, but his long pants made me feel silly. What had seemed right before now seemed out of place. I was ashamed of my short pants and the length of bare leg that showed between the top of the black-ribbed stockings and the pants.

If the earth had offered me a hole to fall into I would have been happy. It seemed there was no escape and that everybody in the village was looking only at me and my cut-down pants. The turned-up edges chafed at my legs and one silly stocking chose that moment to slip down. There was only one thing to do. I pasted Harold and turned tail, fleeing back to the church-shed where Father had left the team.

My father didn't say much at first on the way home. Then he remarked casually, "Saw Harold's mother in the grocery store. Seems Harold had a bit of an accident. Got a black eye."

I didn't say anything. When we crossed the river bridge he said, "Better tell me about it before she gets on the telephone to your mother."

So I told him about my shame over the short pants. He grunted something and said he would do what he could with my mother over the pants problem. He must have warded off the punishment for the incident on Main Street: I waited a week and my mother didn't mention it.

My problem with short pants grew into a real bugbear. I was determined to get rid of them at any cost. I thought of hiding them. Once I even thought of burning them.

My first act in the campaign was to refuse to go to church wearing the short pants. Mother wept a little and said I was only a child and Father gave me a boot on the seat of my pants.

I had to find a campaign with more subtlety. I started remembering all the boys with long pants. At the dinner table I would suddenly remember a certain boy who had just acquired a suit with not one . . . no, sir . . . not one . . . but *two* pairs of long pants.

"Is that so?" Mother would say indifferently, and, just to add insult to injury she would add, "Why, he's a good twenty months older than you. Goodness, I suppose in a year or so we'll have to get you long pants for Sunday."

Time somehow eased the pain of wearing short pants. I grew taller and the space between the pants and the stocking tops grew wider.

Then one day, Father took me into town and on the way in he gave me a long lecture about education. It seemed that just because I had passed my entrance was no reason for me to give up school.

We stopped at Jim Medd's tailor shop. Medd was a very small bespectacled man with a sharp face, who looked as if he might have made clothes for the wee folk. This time he was a magical figure as he fitted me for a coat and, of all things, a vest. I couldn't bear even to think what would happen if I had to wear a vest with short pants, but there was hanging over my head the knowledge that Mother was convinced I should have at least one bought suit with short pants before graduating to long ones.

The little tailor grinned and stroked his moustache and asked, "Long or short pants, son?"

My tongue froze into a lump in my mouth. I couldn't get a word out at all. My father looked grim for a minute and then smiled in a way that unfroze my heart as he said, "Long ones, Jimmy. The boy's gettin' on to be a man."

In the happy, pre-bathing suit days there was an unwritten law around our place that the folks didn't question us on a hot, Sunday afternoon when we announced that we were going back to the river. There was a word or two of caution about being careful, but they weren't serious. Everybody was too full of Sunday dinner and thoughts of napping to really worry.

A country costume for a small boy consisted of a pair of overalls and a shirt. Sometimes the shirt was dispensed with. One of my darkest moments came the Sunday I forget to take off my underwear when I removed my suit after coming from church. When I arrived at the swimming-hole behind the Higgins' place some boys were in the water and others were in the process of shucking their shirts and overalls. When the hollering started I remembered I was in my underwear. You could hear the hoorawing for a mile. I was revealed as a sissy.

Consternation made me stand as if frozen to the spot. I wasn't even aware of the boys' panic as they jumped into the water to a decent point of immersion. A moment later the main-liner streaked by and I threw myself into the water, underwear and all. I didn't realize that the underwear was a godsend until the township constable happened to stop on the sideroad as I splashed in. When he called out, "Glad to see you boys are wearing suits," it at least calmed down my tormentors.

When the Hendersons had their two city nieces at the farm one summer, they decided to have a Sunday afternoon lawn party. I wasn't quite certain what a lawn party was but I had seen the nieces. They were twins, about the prettiest-looking girls I had ever seen outside of a magazine. Knowing that the Higgins children had already been invited, I waited a week of anxious eternity wondering if I would be, too.

Joe Higgins reminded me every day of the fact that the Hendersons had the biggest ice-cream freezer in the township. Recalling it now, I wonder if my ardour was for the ice-cream or the twins. I hadn't really much hope of being invited, anyhow, because my father and Henderson had had a disagreement over the selling of a horse and weren't speaking.

After church, however, Mrs. Henderson asked my mother if I could come for the party about two o'clock in the afternoon. This gave Mother the right to scrub my ears and face and make me wear a pair of knickers, a white shirt, long black stockings and a freshly-shined pair of high boots.

I was warned to take the concession road and not go through

the fields. A boy had to have some pride and I knew a short-cut. A new stretch of barbed wire in a neighbouring field caused me some anxiety and I did get hung up on it, but managed to unsnarl myself. There didn't seem to be any damage so I headed on to the Hendersons.

The lawn party was exactly what its name suggested. About twenty of the children from school looked at each other self-consciously until Mrs. Henderson arrived and suggested games. The girls had to choose partners for "drop the handkerchief" and fortune was riding high in the sky for me. The twin called Elsie came over and led me, blushing and confused, to the circle. The embarrassment vanished when we became immersed in the game.

Joe Higgins was caught and as he passed behind me he whispered, "How did you get that hole in your pants?" In confusion I begged off the game and took a seat on the veranda. Everybody wanted to get me to play but I blushed and sat firm.

Mrs. Henderson was a woman of discernment. She shepherded me into the kitchen and produced needle and thread.

There are poses more conducive to romance than to find oneself over the capacious lap of a woman sewing up a hole in the seat of your pants. When a golden-haired girl appeared on the scene, I was mortified. My embarrassment lasted only until the ice-cream and cake arrived.

One day Father stopped the team at the schoolhouse at late recess and asked the teacher to let me out early. It was unusual for him to do this. The horses were pointed in the direction of the village and there were some grain bags in the back of the democrat. I knew enough not to ask what he had in mind.

After a mile or so of jogging along, he finally spoke:

"Your aunt is coming in on the five o'clock train from the city."

My reply of "Oh!" sounded faint in the outdoors. I was still puzzled as to why I had been commandeered for the trip. The mystery was solved in another mile when he spoke again, and handed me a twenty-five-cent piece.

"Your mother wants you to get a haircut at Jake's."

Then I fretted all the way to town about my first visit to a barber shop. Prior to this I had been exposed to my father's clipping with scissors and shears and a bowl on my head as a guide. All too soon we stopped in front of the little white building with the false façade and the big front window with its display of geraniums.

"I'm leaving the grain at the grist mill and picking up your aunt. If you get finished before that I'll meet you at the store."

He drove off down the street, leaving me alone and very nervous in front of the shop. It was like opening a new and unknown chapter of my life to push open the barber-shop door with the jangling bell and walk in.

I didn't see anything as I slid onto the nearest chair. A little man with a green eye-shade stood behind the barber chair cutting the Presbyterian minister's hair.

"Afternoon. You Bill's boy?"

I half gulped and mumbled an affirmative reply.

"What's your name?"

"Uh . . . Harry."

The little man then did something that endeared him to me for life.

"I'm Jake. Only one ahead of you. Like to see the funnies?"

I nodded and eagerly grasped the magical pages of coloured funnies. Comic strips from the Sunday papers were a great luxury in those days.

There were the sounds of shears snipping, a kettle bubbling on the old pot-bellied stove at the rear of the shop, the shuffling of feet as two old men, puffing on pipes, silently played checkers, and the never-ending drone of Jake's conversation.

I was shocked when I looked up in the big mirror and found that the old minister had his eyes closed. Once or twice his head slipped away from the shears and he snorted into wakefulness. He was finally finished and Jake helped him into his fur coat and funny fur hat. The minister paid Jake and then handed me a five-cent piece from the change. I determined not to mention it at home. My father and mother wouldn't mind but Grandfather would probably reason that the minister was trying to buy a Sunday School member.

A drover, who was the man next in line, put his cigar on the edge of the shelf under the mirror. This was the first time I had watched a man being shaved except for two or three peeks from the sidewalk. Jake moved about on his small feet as if he were afraid of breaking eggs, lathering and towelling in a swinging, swirling sort of way. The towels were steaming hot.

Then there was another lathering and the razor glided like new skates on ice as he removed the whiskers.

The five-cent piece burned in my pocket beside the quarter. I felt guilty for accepting it. My turn came just as the clerk from Murphy's store came in. I walked apprehensively to the chair. Jake was puzzled. I was too big to sit on the board across the arms of the chair and when I sat in the chair the back of it came up too high for Jake to cut my hair. He put me on a tall stool and draped a white sheet around me.

"Shave?" inquired the little barber reaching for the brush and mug.

"A haircut, please," I almost screamed.

That was Jake's joke. He chuckled, the clerk laughed and the two old men looked up for a few moments before going back to their game. I was too young for Jake's soliloquy so he addressed it to the clerk, who now and again looked up from a pink paper called *The Police Gazette* and grunted.

Then I saw the sign. Haircuts for grown-ups were twenty-five cents and for children the price was fifteen cents. I puzzled over whether he would charge me as a grown-up or as a child, and wished I had worn short pants instead of overalls. Then I remembered that my stockings were rolled up to my knees over the pant legs.

The last act of the haircut was a drenching in a tonic with a high scent. I handed Jake the twenty-five cents. He put it in his pocket and helped me on with my coat. Then he reached in his sweater pocket and handed me ten cents.

Even my aunt's complaining about having to ride in the democrat and Father's disgust with the smell of what he called the "sheep-dip" on my hair, couldn't take away from the genuinely wonderful feeling of that memorable afternoon when I had my first "boughten" haircut.

When I approached adolescence, I wanted to fit into a man's world. I came by it slowly at first and then seemed catapulted into it. Driving the team and plowing by myself; driving stock to the station for shipment; attending a nomination meeting with Father at the township hall—all these were steps. Then one day, I was allowed to go to a threshing in place of Father, who was busy.

I can still remember when I was told to go up in the mow that first time. In practically no time I could scarcely see the man I was pitching the sheaves at. The dust and the barley awns and the thistles were clouding the air like a dirty fog. As the initial pleasure of doing the work of a man decreased my muscles began to ache. My nose was stuffed up with a combination of mucus and dust and my throat was parched. Even the water pail which was passed around from time to time didn't help much, because in no time flat the surface of the water was covered with dust and dirt and when I tried to skim it off, I only succeeded in stirring up the whole mess into the consistency of mud.

Noticing the other men chewing tobacco I remembered the advice of my grandfather, who maintained that chewing tobacco was the only thing that would cut dust. I asked Jack Henderson for a chew. He looked startled, but grinning through his mask of dirt, he handed me the plug.

"Better not swallow it," he yelled, taking back the plug after I had gnawed a bite from it.

At first it was fine. It was a novelty and I remembered that you couldn't get sick from tobacco if you were working in the mow. The sheaves were slippery and not too well mowed. My foot slipped, the fork flew—and down went the juicy cud of tobacco into an unhappy stomach.

Five minutes later I crawled from the mow. Ten minutes later I was ardently praying for death, gasping in the shade of the water tank. Something went wrong with the separator and the men piled out for a breath of air. This was one time I couldn't blush. My face was too chalky for even a faint flush. Between gasps I could see the ring of grinning faces and I knew then that there were many dark moments ahead on the road to manhood.

16

SUNDAYS

SUNDAYS WERE DIFFERENT FROM OTHER days on the farm. We went to church in the morning. Most of the neighbours went in the afternoon or the evening. This made it difficult for me to find concession playmates, and as a result, I spent a lot of time at home, alone.

Grown-ups, as I recall now, always seemed to act rather strangely on the Sabbath. The feeling that Sunday was not an ordinary day came in the first dawning hours when I realized that I could sleep longer than on week-days. Grandfather, either through force of habit, or because of his afternoon or early evening snoozes in the rocker, got up at his regular time. He always stomped a bit louder than usual and Father groaned protestingly from his bedroom.

Lying in bed I felt the lure of the summer morning in the

way the curtains bosomed out with the early morning air pushing at them. Flannelette sheets that felt so warmly soothing during the chilly nights now felt a bit tacky. Soon I could smell the aroma of Grandfather's pipe tobacco. The blue smoke came up by the side of the house, slithering in to tantalize me.

Dressing was an easy matter. I slipped into overalls and a shirt and then padded as quietly as possible down the front stairs. Fear of being caught and sent back to bed made me cautious. Those stairs were enemy territory. Hostile ears were waiting to hear a revealing squeak. Bare feet had to be placed just so along the outside edges of the steps. The centre always creaked.

The hours of early warmth before the day had really begun were Grandfather's. I think he used to dream of his own spring-time and early summer. Blood, sluggish with the years, must have moved more quickly under the almost sensual caress of the warm, morning air.

As a concession to the day Grandfather wore his better boots because the best ones reposed in tissue paper in a bureau drawer, saved, I suppose, for the Day of Judgment. He held his suit pants up with a pair of suspenders that looked like harness traces. He had a white shirt with a black pin stripe but no collar, only a gold stud. Collars were worn only for the weddings of close relatives. He did a few minor chores in the morning, and then shaved, spluttering water in a vain attempt to keep lather from his shirt and trousers. The last step was to polish his boots to a startling black with liquid stove polish. This polish, rapidly acquiring dust particles, was strangely grey by church-time.

After breakfast, wearing his suit coat and a felt hat, he waited in the rocker. There was always a note of censure for the rest of the family in the firm way he rocked. It was apparent that the family was responsible for keeping him from church.

Sunday morning for Father was a time of indecision. Weekday mornings he was a general in action. On Sundays he was off-duty, and spent a great deal of time yawning and scratching, forgetting things and grumbling softly to himself about the rigours of his life and work.

"Damn the chores!" summed up his general Sunday

morning philosophy, as if they were something that should be excluded from Sunday routine.

We always had something different for Sunday morning breakfast. Often it was pancakes. I can still picture the blue smoke from the pan and brown-gold cakes being stacked up and demolished as rapidly as they appeared, along with copious quantities of our own home-made butter and the richest of home-made maple syrup. That syrup, brown and golden, tasted like the essence of all the good experiences of my life.

We had other treats. Fresh side pork would be fried and accompanied by fried apple slices, perky with cinnamon and honey. The pork, fried and put away diligently in its own lard in crocks, brought forth and heated was as good as any candy. Well, almost as good! There were eggs, of course, at all times.

The clanging of the clock brought the dawdle at the breakfast table to a close. Grandfather paused in his rocking to say, "Are we going to church or not?" This was the signal for the rush.

The main battle of the morning for me was the bout at the wash basin. Try as I might, I could never get by my mother. To be honest, I always wanted to be clean. I never revelled in dirt but grown-ups make it hard for a growing boy to be clean on his own. I think they would have been disappointed if they hadn't been able to pounce on a dirt-crusted ear or neck.

"Did you wash your neck?"

Now, it didn't matter how hygienically the neck had been washed. Clean or not, that neck and those ears would be subjected to the tightly twisted corner of a towel, poking like a wet wooden finger into every nook and cranny. Hands were dipped and scrubbed vigorously and then dried with a flourish. Mother's moment of triumphant inspection came to a close with a toot from the horn of the old Model T Touring.

Grandfather moved towards the lane gateway. I lingered in the doorway and Mother fussed while Father fumed.

"Is your mother coming?"

I relayed the question.

"I'll be there in a minute."

Mother rushed and fussed. Windows and doors that remained open all week whether we were at home or not had to be closed and locked. The church envelopes, carefully put out on Saturday night, had vanished from sight. A hat had to be adjusted and a scarf found.

I cadged cookies and relayed the messages. Father would blow the horn in an irritated manner and Mother, red-faced, would slam the kitchen door.

"Blow that horn once more and you'll go to church by yourself."

Father didn't reply. We scooted out the front gateway and waited for Grandfather to close the gate. Then we were off in earnest. Mother clung to her hat, Grandfather smoked like a steamer and Father, his arm draped over the steering wheel, with his thorny thumbs cocked for gas lever and spark looked like a speed driver.

I always got hungry on the way to church and nibbled cookies, while we rattled on with side curtains flapping on a pleasant Sunday morning.

I always hoped we would either have company or else go away on Sunday afternoon. This was simply because I dreaded the quiet slumbering of a Sunday afternoon when the family was alone, especially in the summer-time.

The routine never seemed to vary in the good old days. We came home from church and after putting the car in the driving-shed, there were a few simple chores to be done, such as feeding the pigs and the calves and gathering the eggs. Then Father strolled down to take a look at a field of ripening grain or, perhaps, after whistling for the collie he walked through the root patch or examined the corn for signs of borer.

What to do? That was a big question for a boy not considered old enough to hike away by himself to the swimming-hole in the river, or even walk across the fields to visit his cousin on the sideroad.

My parents didn't object to my walking almost two miles to school, but Sunday afternoon was always considered different.

As a boy I was allowed to keep my good clothes on after church, but was constantly reminded to be careful. If I tried to change them, I was told not to, because "somebody might drop in."

There was an old buggy tire to roll as a hoop but after a try it seemed pretty silly in the face of such a general air of listlessness. An attempt to build a fortification of clay in the dirt beside the back stoop brought a rap on the window, and a general warning to keep my clothes clean.

Finally I heard the dinner bell. Grandfather came awake from his old rocker on the side veranda and Father came up the laneway, stopping only to wash his hands at the basin on the old bureau that served as an outdoor washstand in the summertime.

The great platter of roast chicken, the mashed potatoes and the gravy bowl of thick, rich goodness made my mouth water. There were pickles and green lettuce in a bowl with a dash of sugar and vinegar on them. The bread, baked on Saturday afternoon, was cut thick and it was still soft. This was followed by fresh strawberries or raspberries, or the big blackberries I had helped to pick on Saturday morning in the burned-over slash beside the old sawmill.

Maybe it was the general indolence of the day that made me eat so much. Maybe it was the fact that there was little conversation, and the sounds at the table were mostly of eating.

Grandpa moved to his rocker for a smoke and a rock and pretty soon his head dropped and he was fast asleep, with ashes slithering down his already well decorated vest. Mother put the dishes out in the back kitchen and then vanished into the front of the house. I knew she was going to lie down almost stiffly on the spare bed for "forty winks" that would stretch into the greater part of the afternoon.

Father sometimes took to the old couch on the side veranda and pretty soon he was sound asleep, too.

What to do? I watched the flies playing games on Father's face and his slapping at them in a semi-conscious way. I listlessly watched Grandfather, waiting for that inevitable moment when his pipe went clattering to the floor.

Generally I made use of the spare time to investigate the front parlour, a domain which was out of bounds unless the family had company. There were the old pictures, all faded pinkish or brown, of a dreary succession of men with moustaches and whiskers and women with hair that was piled up on their heads like beehives.

There was a book about the Boer War and a collection of stereopticon slides for the stereopticon, but I soon tired of viewing Victoria Falls, Niagara Falls and Smiths Falls. I sat back and listened to the lazy, droning scramble of the big blue flies that always seemed to inhabit the space between the drawn, green blinds and the windows in the spare room.

How glad I was to hear Father tramping upstairs in the late afternoon. The resolute sound informed me that the lull was over and that he was going to change into his working clothes and I could follow suit.

I knew that Father might even be game for a trip to the "other place" to salt the cattle. In fact, I also knew that after the chores he might be induced to go back and take a skinny dip in the river.

Best of all, I knew that the slow, ticking hours of a lazy summer Sunday afternoon were over for another week.

17

WONDERFUL GRANDPARENTS

GRANDPA HAD NONDESCRIPT HAIR THAT LOOKED LIKE shredded wheat, and a red beard that wind, weather and chewing tobacco had stained, but when I looked closely there were some wonderful wrinkles at the corners of his eyes. Those eyes, blue but a little faded, could convey to a youngster subjected to parental wrath a comforting warmth of feeling.

Grandmother was big-bosomed and bulky in a black dress, but her hair was snowy white and she always seemed to have just put on a freshly starched apron. Her face was pink and white and she had a habit of brushing at the loose strands of white hair that never seemed to stay in place over her ears. Grandfather always seemed to have a piece of horehound candy in his pocket and Grandmother had a sixth sense for knowing when a glass of lemonade and fresh gingerbread cookies did the most good for a growing boy.

Grandparents always seemed to live in such interesting places. There were plenty of those old-fashioned rocking chairs and a glider on the front porch and a hammock in the backyard. I suppose these furnishings would be considered old-fashioned nowadays but they were mighty comfortable when I was a boy.

The kitchen was big and dominated by an enormous range. The place always seemed to smell of spices and cooking. On a Sunday afternoon, peering through the illustrated book of pictures from the Boer War, I stopped and listened to the medley of sounds. Grandfather snored gently on the old sofa that had the pillows filled with cedar twigs. The old clock with the gaily painted face ticked ceremoniously away, as a sort of counter-rhythm to the gently protesting squeak of the rocker that Grandmother favoured, which nudged imperceptibly across the floor as she rocked. The tea-kettle burbled in a fat-bellied, jolly way while the fat old tabby on the rag rug in front of the stove wheezed with comfortable age.

In those days all grandparents seemed to be interesting people. I suppose it was their years of the trials and tribulations of raising a family that endowed grandparents with a charm all their own. On one point they were all alike. They couldn't see any harm in what their grandchildren did.

Their indulgent attitude sometimes stood me in good stead. I remember one particular day when I was plodding home from school. There was a sewing circle meeting at the church on the concession and Miss Binkley's grey mare was tied to the fence. The older boys started joshing me about my courage and I was young and foolish enough to give in and switch wheels on the buggy. It was an old-fashioned one with larger wheels on the back so I switched a front one for a back one, giving the buggy a slightly uneven gait.

We all hid in a patch of burdock by the church shed and watched Miss Binkley come out, prim as a cucumber and sour as a chokecherry. She started off and the buggy went bumpety-wow . . . bumpety-wow. . . . The horse twisted his tail, whinnied angrily and snorted, then took off, with Miss Binkley hanging on to the dashboard. Her bonnet flew off and suddenly the joke lost its flavour. I sneaked home as fast as two bare feet could make it over a freshly gravelled road.

I didn't eat much supper and Mother wanted to send me to bed. In fact, I think I was developing a first-class fever. When the telephone rang I lit out for the home of my grandparents on the next concession. They looked a little surprised at my arrival and even more surprised when I wouldn't eat a piece of fresh, raspberry pie.

There were a few questions which I managed to duck and then they wisely let the matter drop. The twilight took an intolerably long time to fade away. I sat with Grandfather on the veranda while he smoked his pipe and told me a few stories about some escapades he had had as a young man. Time wore on and he recounted some familiar stories about the lumber woods.

I was just going to ask him if I could stay all night when he suggested that he drive me home.

"Your mother will be worrying about you, lad," he said gently.

The horror of the whole situation mounted every moment. I would catch it for the incident of the buggy wheels, because even at that age I realized that there was little loyalty in the crowd that had egged me on to the mischief. The whole affair would be aggravated by the fact that I had gone away from home for the first time without telling my parents where I was going.

Wild schemes of escape began to sort themselves out in my mind. There was a freight that went through the village about ten o'clock and I thought I might hop on it and go far away. For a few seconds I felt relieved, but sober reality chased that away. There was also the matter of the six dollars that I had in my dresser drawer at home; but there was little chance of getting that without being apprehended. I had finally decided on the old shack down by the river on the McCabe farm, when Father drove down the laneway.

I ducked behind the chair where my grandfather was sitting. My father was in a rage and he made a lunge for me, but Grandfather restrained him and Grandmother arrived on the scene to help calm him. As I had expected, the other boys had turned informers.

"What would you do with a boy like that?" stormed my father. "Is he going to the bad?"

Grandfather stopped to light his pipe and I could see his moustache twitching in the flaring light of the match.

"If somebody had pulled a few tricks on that old maid twenty-five years ago, she wouldn't be so sour now," he said slowly as he flicked the match away.

Father sat down and in reply to Grandpa's questioning

explained how the horse had been caught by the blacksmith in town. Grandfather started to talk then.

"Remember the time you tied the can to the tail of the preacher's dog and he slammed into church in the middle of the Thompson wedding, when Alice was marrying that city fellow, and they had had everything rigged up by some big outfit from Toronto?"

He paused then and finally said, "I was going to whale the tar out of you until my father reminded me of the time I put the rat in the teacher's desk and she fainted."

My father was quiet on the way home but he chuckled once or twice as if remembering something funny. Before we turned in the laneway he said, "You don't have to fib about this but it wouldn't hurt if you let your mother think I tanned your backside."

I had a wonderful feeling for the patience of my parents that night when I finally went to bed, but I sure said a large-sized prayer for my grandparents and thanked the Lord for that wonderful belief they had about a grandchild's doing no wrong.

Grandfather had an amazing streak of pride in his make-up. There was, for instance, the case of the portrait.

Now and again a travelling artist made the rounds of the township, painting portraits from photographs. He was a friendly chap and a good talker and knew enough to arrive at people's houses a little before the dinner-hour. He always said he wanted to pay for his meal, but never did. The folks used to say he never would unless they set the farm dog on him.

Just how the artist managed to talk Grandfather into having an enlarged portrait made was always a sort of puzzle. He found an old picture of Grandfather in the family album and at once got lost in admiration; it looked for a while as though he had gone into a trance or something like that. He was full of one of Mother's good meals when he tackled Grandfather and his sales pressure was running high. He even walked around the parlour and pointed to a spot by the organ where the easel, which went with the picture, would stand. I guess Grandfather could almost see the thing in place and realized it would add some class to the room, so his name went down on the dotted line and the travelling artist departed with Grandfather's photograph.

It was a good three or four weeks before he came back, with the whole works tied up in a bundle riding in the buggy beside him. No person in the house was allowed to run out and bring it in. The artist himself handled it with great care; in fact he almost fondled it as though it were dear to him. He said he would have dinner first and then unveil it with all the members of the family properly seated in the parlour. He said a little ceremony like that got the thing off to a good start and furnished one of those long-to-be-remembered moments, something like the time we won first prize on mangels at the fall fair.

The easel was made out of pieces of bamboo which the artist said were especially imported. He shoved chairs around a little and got the easel and the big, framed picture in place and then took off the piece of newspaper he had over it. That was the unveiling, but the travelling artist did so much bowing and scraping that it seemed like quite an occasion.

There was Grandfather in a frame over two feet high and a good foot and a half across. Everyone admitted it was a dandy frame. Those were the days when the gold standard was working more than eight hours a day. It may have been gilt but it knocked the spots off everything else in the room and made the painted shade on the hanging lamp look kind of shabby.

After the company had looked at the frame, they began looking at Grandfather. Some person tittered, which seemed to annoy the artist. He took Grandfather first to one angle of vision and then another and explained just what a great work of art it was. You could tell, by looking at it closely, that it was Grandfather but there was something strange about it. His ears had always been large but in the picture they looked bigger than ever and the artist had neglected to shove them back. There was a rather wild look in the left eye which would have been out of place in the family pew on Sunday morning.

There was no law suit. Grandfather was a stickler for doing what he had agreed upon. About the time of the spring house-cleaning the enlarged photo came down off the easel and one of Queen Victoria took its place. Grandfather's picture was put up in the spare bedroom, and he drove the nail in the wall himself. He never actually complained about the picture, but in one of his rare spells of humour he remarked that with his picture in the spare room company would probably not be inclined to overstay their welcome.

My grandfather always enjoyed thunderstorms. He sat calmly on the back veranda and watched the clouds rolling up over the skyline, happy because they were black and boiling and a sure sign of a storm.

I can still remember the little gusts of wind that spun eddies of dust in the laneway. They were mischievous zephyrs that flapped the curtains through the open windows, dashed the papers from the sideboard and rippled the loose shingles on the back woodshed. They were a warning to my mother, who dashed through the house pulling out the screens and slamming down the windows.

Grandfather stayed on the veranda in the old rocking chair. The smoke from his pipe curled up, escaping through the spot in the veranda roof where the shingles had rotted. By the time Mother had the windows down, the first, big splattering drops of rain were falling and Grandfather moved his chair.

I liked to sit beside him when a storm was brewing in the west. After the first tentative drops, the rain came sluicing down, to be sucked up by the ground, while the war drums of thunder sounded off in the distance. There was a misty, steamy quality in the air.

That was one type of storm when the rain came but the thunder and lightning stayed at a distance. The real dramatic ones were those that began with thunder in the distance and a darkening sky. My grandfather enjoyed this type even more than the other ones. He always reminded me that he had said at the supper table, the evening before, that we were bound to get this storm. After I had absorbed this information without any argument, he took his pipe out and leaned forward in the chair, indicating with the smoking pipe a spot in the sky.

With the dignity of an ancient prophet he said, "Lad, she'll break about there."

Mother hovered inside the screen door and scolded us for staying outside. I was safe as long as Grandfather stayed on the veranda. Every so often my mother would peer out at the field behind the barn, or wherever my father was working and say, "I can't understand for the life of me why that man doesn't unhitch the team and come to the barn."

The storm progressed. The clouds rolled deeper and

darker and the thunder growled loudly. Jagged flashes of lightning danced jigs on the shoulders of distant hills.

About the time my father got to the barn there was a blinding bolt of lightning that seared the sky, followed by a tremendous roll of thunder. The rain came in gigantic spurts and the storm closed in as if it were trying to smother our farm. Great blasts of thunder rattled the windows and the sharp cracking of the lightning sounded like a circus master's whip, the black clouds like sulky lions pacing the enormous cage of the sky. The storm was on!

Mother's voice suddenly got an edge on it. She was not to be trifled with when she said, "Get in here—both of you!" Grandfather got up, tucked the cushion under one arm and for a few moments he put his hand out to feel the rain sluicing down the veranda roof. He loved the rain. I think my father did, too, because he always managed to get soaked on his way up from the barn. When Mother scolded him, he grinned and said, "Rain's good for you. Makes your hair grow."

A storm always brought out the coward in Aunt Minnie. She arranged her chair so as to be as far as possible away from the chimney, the doors and the windows. There she sat, plucking at her hands and fussing all the time the storm was on. Sometimes she went to her room where, Grandfather maintained, she hid under the bed.

About the time the storm was at its peak, my grandfather started telling stories about the bad storms he had known. It made my skin creep to hear the yarns about times when he saw great balls of fire burst out of stoves and chimneys and chase people around the room.

His masterpiece concerned a ball of lightning that, as he said, "just zoomed around the room twice and landed in a corner. Something like that corner Minnie is sitting in." About that time Aunt Minnie gasped and squealed and Grandfather bided his time until an extra-loud roll of thunder came along. Then he said, "That bolt of lightning just seemed to explode into bits and it blew the corner clear out of the room." As a dramatic afterthought he added, "They never found that fellow again . . . the one sitting in the corner."

Grandfather certainly enjoyed storms. But then, you see, Minnie was from the other side of the family and Grandfather was never overly fond of her anyway.

18
SCHOOL DAYS

JUNE DAYS WERE ALWAYS DREAMY DAYS IN school. The windows were open and the air filled with the lazy, droning sound of birds and insects and the far-away clittery-clattery sound of a mower in June hay. The occasional wind sprite sighed through the old pines in the schoolyard, then slipped into the room, bringing the tantalizing smells of weeds and new-mown hay and some vague essence that could be called "summeriness."

I moped through the morning session. Classes were unimportant because the examinations were over and my fate had been decided for the coming year. I was there because of some vague thing called the school rules and regulations and Mr. Crombe. Mr. Crombe had never been blessed with children but he had Mrs. Crombe, who made certain that he stayed as a school trustee for seventeen years to ensure that the life was hounded out of every schoolteacher in our district. They made a particular personal triumph of seeing that the last day was observed. Regular as clockwork every year, Mr. and Mrs. Crombe drove past the school to see that we were doing our duty.

The blackboards were washed and the teacher got out her coloured chalk and drew on the board a tableau of children, birds, flowers and bees. In rolling penmanship, she wrote "HAPPY HOLIDAYS." This heightened the tension because we knew that she was weakening and wanted to let us go. When we saw the Miller boy drive slowly by the school with his horse and buggy, it could only mean that he was driving her to the village to catch the train. Since they had been going steady for two years it was reasonable to assume that he wouldn't dash for the four-twenty-five train without allowing a little time to spark.

Desk contents were re-assorted and then packed in school bags and put out on the desk again. The teacher read a story but that lasted for only ten minutes. We stared at the pictures of the King and Queen, somewhat faded with age, and then lost ourselves in the monstrous picture called "Watch On The Rhine" given the school by the patriotic Daughters of the Empire. The Boer War pictures showed grinning savages and Boers surrounding a brave British battalion, but it was in black and white and the technicoloured advantages of the other one commanded the majority of attention.

Desks squeaked and rattled. Feet shuffled and there was an incessant and ragged round of unnecessary coughing. The old box stove, grinning with black, polished satisfaction, looked as if it were waiting for the winter when it would again alternately burn and freeze us, in retaliation for the twenty-two caps which were exploded in its depths from time to time. The zinc water pail had been emptied and dried and left demurely beside the upturned tin dipper, setting off a chain reaction of demands for refreshment from thirsty pupils. Chalk and paper and the limited assortment of laboratory equipment was locked in a cupboard because some of the older boys had, on occasion, paid illegal visits to the school during the summer holidays.

Around eleven thirty when the tension had become almost unbearable, the teacher distributed the confiscated articles of the season. There were bull's-eye marbles and slingshots, a harmonica that someone had tootled during school hours and once even the brush from a cow's tail that Joe Willy Jamieson had been using to torture the girls.

At eleven forty-five we had to sweep the school, throwing up a dust screen that set everybody coughing. It looked as though we would be stuck for noon hour, but somehow or other we kept our hope intact. There was a desire to yell when the Crombe buggy came in sight. The teacher grabbed a book, and had a ragged reading of "Indian Summer" by the older boys and girls in voices that could be heard on the next concession.

The Crombes had no sooner vanished over the hill than the Miller buggy pulled up. In a final attempt to channel our energies the teacher made us sing "God Save the King" and "O Canada." Then she hastily wished us a happy holiday and dismissed us. Everybody streaked for home, making certain to cut through the fields in order to escape the Crombe place.

The strange part of it was that a week later, some of us, although we wouldn't admit it, would have gone back to school gladly in order to escape the monotonous drudgery of hoeing turnips or bugging potatoes.

When I went to that school the mark of accomplishment and progress had to do with initials on one's desk. When I started to school I was naturally shy and sat in the front row under the eyes of the teacher. About the middle of the term I got up enough nerve to scratch an initial or two in an inconspicuous place.

By the time I reached junior third and was halfway to the back in the row of seats, I openly cut my initials in the desk top. A few days before the close of the term I carefully inked the initials. The annual coat of varnish put on by the caretaker preserved them in perpetuity.

Having attained the entrance class there was very little I wouldn't do, or at least try. Size gave me the right to sit in the back row of seats, occupying the one nearest the window in summer and the box stove in the winter. A jack-knife being standard equipment for a growing boy in the country, I proceeded to carve the edge of the top board of the desk. After a few years the edge of the desk looked like some of the fancy-work along the eaves of Victorian homes.

The school, having been built by a barn-framer, had all the qualities of a barn. It was hot in summer and frigid in winter. Ventilation came from the warped floors in the winter-time and from the open windows in the summer-time. At recess we filled our pockets with pebbles and between last recess and four o'clock, devoted our energies to throwing them out of the open window, trying not to attract the attention of the teacher.

During the winter season, the after-the-last-recess period was devoted to marksmanship of a different nature. Paper chewed up into spitballs was propelled by means of rulers in the general direction of the ceiling. The younger students just let fly but the older ones had great pride in their skill.

Being caught meant sitting in the darkest corner with one's face to the blackboard, staying in at recess or, if the teacher wasn't in a hurry, after four, or writing out five hundred times, "I have been bad and promise to be good."

Asking to leave the room was a matter of skill. Most teachers forbade more than one pupil to be out of the room at the same time. Now and again I was able to foil her. I waited until my chum had been gone for three or four minutes, and she was busy with a class in front of the room. I then grimaced as if in pain and shot my hand up, waving it like someone going down for the last time. Quite often she would absent-mindedly give me permission to leave. After tittering and giggling in satisfaction outside for five or ten minutes, my friend and I came back singly, never together.

The box stove was a monstrous affair. A member of the school board, having had an old box stove which his wife made him replace with a Quebec heater, palmed it off on the school board for five dollars. Always anxious for a bargain, they bought it, because it "threw such a good heat." It took blocks of wood as long as a threshing machine and consumed them at about the same rate. It scorched everybody within five feet, while the rest of the occupants of the room existed in a semi-frozen state. It sifted ashes at every joint. The only cheerful thing about it was the sight of the dancing flames through the broken door on a day when visibility was poor.

Going down to the store for a pail of water was a chore at home and a pleasure during school hours. Water, needless to say, went at a great rate. There was a general understanding that when you took a drink of water, you filled the dipper and threw the remainder after your drink in the old pail under the table. It was a pleasure to go for a drink and find the pail was empty and then hold up your hand and say, "Please, teacher, there's no water here." On the other hand there were few more bitter feelings than when she said, "All right, you can sit down," and then named somebody else to get the water.

There were two heroic types at school. One of them chewed tobacco in school and used his inkwell for a cuspidor. The teacher, stopping to dab her pen in his inkwell one day on her way down the aisle put a stop to that sport. The other hero was a boy with very calloused feet, who started to go barefoot in early spring and maintained it until the first snow came sifting down. He could place a pin in the callous of his big toe, go on working with both hands on his desk and give the girl ahead a terrific jab through the crack between the chair and the front of the desk.

Recreation consisted mostly of smoking in a secluded place. The plutocrats had real tobacco filched from home, but we of the rank and file had to be content with ground up cedar bark in loose cylinders of newspaper. This produced a vile smoke that half-smothered me and brought tears to my eyes. Another sport was to chase the girls with burrs or a wriggling snake on a stick. A form of ball game played with a home-made bat and ball of yarn wrapped around a stone encased in a rough piece of leather was played in the dense weeds of the schoolyard. Other sports included hunting toads, frogs and mice which were introduced to the class in school hours.

19
COUNTRY CHARACTERS

WHEN I WAS GROWING UP, I DIDN'T THINK OF THE many personalities who passed through our township as characters. I have to now, in retrospect. Oddly enough, the automobile has eliminated most of the ones that used to roam the countryside. Tramps, tinkers, travellers, pedlars, book and magazine agents, gypsies, fishmen, nursery salesmen, scamps and scalawags were always bringing colour up and down the concession and sideroads to an otherwise routine way of life.

One day somebody coming from town said Old Ben was in the area. Mother retorted, "There's no use in that old reprobate coming here. I simply don't want anything from him."

Father smiled and said, "Might break his heart. It always seemed to me he was a little stuck on you."

Mother protested and blushed. After dinner she brushed her hair and put on a clean apron.

Sure enough, that afternoon Old Ben, driving his high-wheeled democrat, appeared.

Old Ben was a descendant of the Phoenician traders, by way of Syria. Summer and winter he wore a leather cap and a long, greasy overcoat with a strap buckled around his wrist which he said controlled his rheumatism. His face was a leathery mass of wrinkles with black eyes that glinted and sparkled when he laughed.

The procedure never varied. Mother was determined that she didn't need a thing. Old Ben gave us some sticks of barley candy and asked if he couldn't mend a pot or a kettle. There was always one with a hole in it and Old Ben retired to his van, fixed it neatly and returned it with a packet of needles.

"Just a little present for the kindness of your smile."

The dam was broken and Mother found that she needed some safety pins. A whole array of items would spill over the veranda or, if it were chilly, over the kitchen table. Scissors and pins, yarn and thread, saucepans and muffin tins, toilet water and fancy soap, spices and flavourings, mitts and gloves, colanders and frying pans, knives and cutlery—a treasure trove of curious objects for small boys.

Of course Old Ben stayed for supper and when the dishes were done he handed Father a black cheroot and started talking. I huddled in the corner watching flames turn into golden pictures through the cracks in the kitchen range. The old pedlar talked about big cities, of the place he was born in a far-off sunny country, of oceans he had crossed, and the contrasting meanness and kindness of human beings.

Old Ben slept on a cot in the room over the kitchen with the hired man. He was always gone by daybreak and never waited for breakfast, but I know that he always found a package of sandwiches and some cake and fruit on the front seat of the old van.

The gypsies often came to camp on the river flats. There were dire warnings from our elders about these people because they were "known" to kidnap children. On the way to school we would nervously inspect their encampment, hoping for a glimpse of the white princess held captive. We thought we saw her once, but she turned out to be an albino. Mostly we saw women washing clothes, children chasing dogs and men tinkering with old cars and leading horses off to try for a trade.

Black Mike had a peg leg and he was proud of his profession as a hobo. He would take his place on the back stoop with a plate of food, put a greasy handkerchief across his knees, extract a knife and fork from his pocket and eat with dainty grace. Afterwards he would play the mouth organ with obvious enjoyment and was allowed to sleep in the barn because he didn't smoke.

The nurseryman used to come with many-coloured catalogues. He persuaded Mother and Father that our farm would would be a fairyland of colour, but somehow the shrubs never amounted to much after they were planted.

The stocks-and-bonds salesmen came to sell dreams of prosperity and wealth, and many tin trunks in rural attics still have their share of flossily engraved certificates.

Just the same, we welcomed all these people because they were a change. It was like a sudden opening in the sky that pressed in around our valley, giving a glimpse of an outside world. It was a romantic relief from a working day that began with the sound of the crowing roosters and the morning freight and ended at night with the wind, winter and summer, playing in the old pine trees.

Not all the country eccentrics who came to the farm were travellers. I imagine every community has a couple like Oscar and Ethel. First of all, Oscar inherited a good farm and some mortgages on three other good farms in the township. This was a nice nest egg and Oscar, who had never seemed to care much about money as a younger man, suddenly became money-conscious.

He was so conscious of money, or at least some people said so, that he jilted Judy Murphy, whose father was a tenant farmer, and married Ethel Hendrix. Ethel was no world-beater for looks, but she had inherited ten thousand dollars from her grandfather, and being an only child she was due to get a good one hundred and fifty acres and some mortgages from her parents.

They suited each other. The day they got married they had dinner at the Commercial Hotel in town and didn't even invite the best man and the bridesmaid. That night they drove back to his farm. Their frivolous spending of money on hotel meals was over.

Now, there's no possible reason for anybody to complain about people who are careful with money. In the case of Oscar and Ethel, people wished they would be as close with their advice as they were with their money. Oscar came over the day we bought our first Model T, and by the time he left he had the whole family convinced, as my father said, that we were "going to Hell in a flivver with a stop at the poorhouse."

At the schoolboard meeting Oscar led off with a diatribe about the unfairness of his paying school taxes when he didn't have any children. Ethel then gave a lecture on how badly the schoolteacher was handling the children. One time, at a Women's Institute meeting she even had the nerve to give a lecture on the care and feeding of babies.

Ethel was unusually preoccupied with babies, especially considering that she didn't have any of her own. Oscar also had a great time lecturing fathers on how they should bring up their boys to respect money, their elders and the local minister. The two clergymen, Catholic and Protestant, were young men who liked to play ball or hockey and they often organized games. Oscar was prone to give the impression that the boys were to blame for somehow damaging the prestige of the gentlemen of the cloth.

At first people said that when they had a family of their own, Oscar and Ethel would learn a few things and be too busy to meddle. The years went by and they remained childless. People were earnestly seeking some way of keeping them quiet when an advertising incident happened that closed their free information bureau for good.

This all took place in the days when the travelling public moved at a slow pace and had time to look around. It was then a fad to paint signs on the side of barns. The farmer pocketed ten or twenty dollars and the paint helped preserve the siding.

One day a young man came along and asked Oscar if he might lease the side of the barn nearest the highway and railroad line. Oscar didn't trouble to find out what the sign was about. He demanded and got twenty-five dollars for a year's lease on the side of the barn. He was even considering how, if the barn had been at the corner of the concession and sideroad, he might have rented all four sides. The sign painters proved to be experts. Moreover, they even bought their dinner from Ethel and didn't haggle over the price. Oscar was feeling the elation and glow of a man who has made a good bargain.

When the first coat had dried, the painters went to work again with the actual sign. Gradually, out of the maze of flowing paint and the curlicues of colour there emerged a sign. First of all there was a baby without clothes, pink and happy. Across from it a distinguished bird with a great bill slowly appeared under the hands of the painters. It was a stork—the famous Dr. Stork of baby medicine fame.

Oscar was bewildered at first. He certainly had a foreboding of the uncomfortable consequences of such a sign. He hadn't expected anything of this nature.

Most of the barn signs concerned themselves with feeds, or fencing or various kinds of patent medicines for use on livestock. This was a different matter. He began to wonder what would happen when Ethel appeared on the scene to view the sign.

The sign was soon completed and, sure enough, Ethel arrived just as the painters were initialling their masterpiece. As she came down the laneway, one of the painters told me later, Oscar seemed to shrivel up like a pea in a pod on a hot July day.

The stork and the baby loomed up in front of Ethel. The pair of them, stork and baby, would have been bad enough but there was a commercial message that added insult to injury. This was the salt in the wound. It read in tremendous letters: "Dr. Stork Is Always Welcome In Our Home."

Ethel almost had a seizure. She stormed and raved, demanding that the sign be removed. The painters assured her it couldn't be removed.

Then she demanded that the sign be painted over, hiding baby and stork from the view of the general public. The painters laughed at her, and told Oscar to read his contract. Oscar trotted up to the house while the men were packing their equipment, to the high-voiced accompaniment of Ethel demanding her rights.

It was a crestfallen Oscar who appeared from the house. He had read his contract. It was an ironclad one, saying that the sign had to remain for a year and that the contractor had the right to touch it up if the weather faded the sign.

That sign became a landmark. Conductors on passing trains delighted in telling the passengers the anecdote of the childless couple and the stork. Engineers tooted their whistles at it as they passed by. People dawdled by on Sunday afternoons or had picnics on the far side of the railroad bridge in a spot where they could examine the sign at their leisure.

Oscar was a township councillor and at meetings the reeve loved to ask "Dr. Stork" for his opinion on matters. Mrs. Oscar tried once or twice to offer some advice on parental care at community meetings, but the other women smiled her into silence. Oscar quit the council without running for reeve. He didn't appear at any more meetings of the schoolboard.

The end of that year couldn't come too soon for the couple. Then Oscar was faced with a dilemma. The company wouldn't paint the sign over and Oscar didn't want to paint one side without painting the whole barn, and he was too frugal to do that. He tried scraping the sign off but it was mighty good paint. He tried burning it off and almost set the barn on fire.

Finally, Oscar took the siding off and reversed it, putting the painted side on the inside. Even to this day, at threshing time, men working up in the mow try to decipher the colours, now faded, of the "Dr. Stork" sign.

For as long as I could remember, "Five Aces" Cassidy had been a character in our community. He lived in a rambling, weather-beaten house near the sawmill, carried a cane, wore a battered Stetson hat and a drooping moustache and went to church once a year. The church pilgrimage was on the Sunday nearest to the date of the death of his mother.

When I was a boy there was always a mystery surrounding "Five Aces." His name came from an expression which he used in almost every conversation.

"I feel like I was holding five aces with nothing wild."

The stories were legion about Cassidy. He talked, but when you examined his story he had really said very little about himself. There was a general impression among the youngsters of our village that he had given lessons to Buffalo Bill and Wild Bill Hickock.

In the village we used to see him walking down to the post office to get the paper. He was a tall, slightly stooped figure. We presumed that his stoop came from years of practising a "gun crouch" for a lightning draw. In the summer-time he wore fine, soft, cowboy boots with high heels, grey moleskin pants, a collarless shirt with a gold stud and a vest. In the winter-time he wore a black broadcloth coat that was just over knee-length. His white hair was bunched at the back of his head under the battered grey sombrero.

Sometimes "Five Aces" sat in an arm-chair on the veranda of the Union House. There was always a crowd around and he talked in a slow, continuous drawl. He was a born story-teller and our librarian said, "He's gone through every book we have and some of them three or four times."

Occasionally, if a boy was lucky he might have a chance to see the inside of Cassidy's house. He used only two rooms in the draughty old place. The kitchen was a maze of tin cans, empty biscuit boxes and dirty utensils, with firewood clustered around the old range. He ate from a tin plate set in a small clearing on the corner of the table.

The living-room was dominated by an old cast-iron stove like the one in the depot. His bed was a jumble of blankets on a cot in the corner. There were two or three dilapidated but comfortable chairs. Books and guns lay everywhere. In contrast to the rest of the place, the guns were oiled and polished, although no one had ever seen him use one.

He was a gentle, polite and dignified man. The women were always flattered by his old-fashioned bow and the touch to the hat brim when he met them on the street. The men stood in awe of his amazing vocabulary and "book larnin'." We children were fascinated by his fund of stories of the Old West.

One day when I was putting an ad in the paper for a strayed heifer, "Five Aces" happened to pass by *The Courier* office. Having become a farmer in the district, I hadn't seen the old gentleman in some time and remarked to Jim Parker, the editor, "You know, for a man that has lived such a dangerous life, "Five Aces" keeps his age remarkably well."

Parker, a blunt and outspoken man, snorted, "The most danger he's ever seen was when he slipped on the ice in front of the Union House."

Then he went on to explain that Cassidy, as a young man, had wanted to go to the Western country and his father had forbidden him to go. Cassidy was going anyhow but delayed because his mother was an invalid. The father died and "Five

Aces" cared for his mother. When she died he inherited a substantial income. He had never left our town but had stayed on in the house. Gradually he changed his clothes, appearance and talk. People, with that tolerance that sometimes happens in small towns, had accepted him without question.

My reaction to Parker's story was a mixture of shock and amusement. Meanwhile Cassidy went on with the annual crop of youngsters. For that matter, most grown-ups found it fascinating to listen to him, too.

Then he died. I wondered how Jim Parker would handle the story. It would be something like writing an obituary for Santa Claus. When the paper appeared it told how the old man had been missed at the post office for two mornings. Someone had gone to investigate. They found he had passed away in his sleep. The report went on to say: " 'Five Aces' Cassidy, noted resident of our community for the past many years and famous pioneer of the Western country of Canada and the United States died at his home here Tuesday. He was thought to be niney-five years old. Daniel Cassidy, known as 'Five Aces' for his use of the expression, 'I feel like I was holding five aces with nothing wild,' had an intimate knowledge and association with such famous characters of the frontier as Buffalo Bill Cody, Wyatt Earp, Jesse James and Kit Carson. He will be missed as a raconteur and entertaining story-teller."

I thought that it was one of the kindest and finest obituaries I had ever read.

SUMMER

20
SUMMER ADVENTURES

A COUNTRY BOY WHO WOULD HAVE BEEN TERrified by town traffic, not to mention city traffic, was a bold adventurer in home territory. This was especially true when he had a city cousin visiting. Commonplace or everyday experiences could, with a bit of skilful suggestion, take on the aura of true adventure.

A girl called Margie was the first to come under my bold spell. She was a small, blonde and rather timid child, allowed very little freedom by a semi-invalid mother. She was sent to our place for a summer because her mother, for whom Father had very little use, was sick. My mother had a great affection for the little girl and vowed to "put roses in her cheeks."

At first she sat most of the time on the veranda, perpetually afraid of getting in someone's way. I had been instructed to try and get her to play. I wasn't to introduce any rough games, however. She smiled at each suggestion shyly and stayed in the chair.

"Margie, why don't you run on and play," suggested my mother.

Margie then transferred herself from the back stoop to the bench beside the driving-shed. I brought out in succession the riches of my play equipment. There was an old steering-wheel from a car, bent but quite usable for playing car, a bent steel buggy hoop, three or four barrel staves, a boat carved by Grandfather from a piece of cedar, a sponge-rubber ball, a jack-knife with a broken blade, a cigar box full of coloured stones, two broom handles, a wad of frayed Sunday comics. Yet, nothing seemed to stir the girl.

I confessed my failure to Grandfather. He nodded and said he would get her playing. He vanished at noon, and re-appeared about one thirty carrying a puppy in his arms. Without saying a word he dumped the pup into the little girl's arms. It was absolutely magical to see the change in the child.

She laughed and cried alternately for about a half hour. My mother smiled and beckoned me into the house.

"Marge will be a fine playmate now. You see that child needs to either love or be loved. Poor thing hasn't had much of either."

That changed the whole summer. Marge was game to go anywhere, just as long as she could carry Spots with her. He was a small, runty puppy of indeterminate origin, saved by Grandfather from drowning, but the grand champion of all the canine world couldn't have displaced him in the affections of the little girl.

Even our old collie seemed to sense the situation. He didn't put up any fuss about the pup. The four of us wandered through the fields and the swale and the bush. We played pirates on the raft on the old pond in the pasture, and poked for frogs and toads in the cold, musty darkness of the creek culvert.

I led an adventurous expedition to the gravel pit, and we buried treasure in the old cave on the side of the brickyard hill. I cut willow wands and bent pins for fishing rods and even Margie caught a diminutive chub which Mother, with all solemnity, fried for her breakfast. We climbed the beams in the barn and became infested with barn lice.

At a tender age I could imagine myself as a combination of every hero I had ever heard of. The pools, the valley and the creek became the setting for untold adventures. Something else was happening. Margie, who gave me tribute as the acknowledged leader, was changing a great deal.

I noticed that she no longer clung to the pup, who by this time had developed into a capering, frolicking creature. She climbed trees, fell into the creek and picked suckers from her arms and legs without squealing. She scrambled over rocks, stuffed herself with berries and chokecherries and followed me into the darkest spot of the old cave.

Her face was browning and freckled. Her hands had callouses and the tender feet could even negotiate the gravel-pit stones. She ate with gusto and slept the night through with no trace of the shadows that had haunted her when she first came to our place.

The day she left for the city, I fled to the back of the barn. It would never have done for me to be seen crying. It was out of character for a bold adventurer to cry over a girl.

On occasion during the summer holidays my uncle, who ran the general store, was called away on business. He was an insurance agent, clerk of the school section, commissioner for taking oaths, treasurer of the township, claims adjuster for a fire insurance outfit as well as storekeeper, so that he often had to make trips. When my aunt went with him I was called in to act as storekeeper.

This, of course, was during the time when most people were busy haying or harvesting, and made infrequent trips to the store. They went early in the morning when the dew was still on the ground or in the evening when it was too late for harvest work. Daytime trips were for emergencies. Lack of customers didn't detract from my zeal as a storekeeper.

My uncle always handed me a bottle of soda pop and a chocolate bar when I arrived. This, I believe, was intended to reduce the normal amount of temptation. In addition, my aunt usually had milk and chocolate cake in the ice-box. My needs in the direction of nourishment were adequately looked after.

The store proper was a large square room, about half the

downstairs area of a very large, white brick building. Most of the groceries, dry goods, medicines and harness were in this part. A large, sloping-roofed shed on the side contained flour and feed, heavy hardware, fencing and anything else that wouldn't go in the store.

The basement of the store was another treasure-house. Great round boxes of cheese were aging in a cool, dark section of the cellar. There were crates of oranges and lemons, boxes of raisins and prunes, great oaken casks of vinegar, a barrel of molasses and a great tub of pickles, as well as a keg of old cider.

In a shed outside the store there were barrels of coal oil, a drum of naphtha gasoline for the Coleman lamps which were coming into favour in our hydro-shy community and open containers of axle grease. Motor oil was in great drums, numbered to indicate the grade for winter or summer use. Outside the shed stood a gaunt-looking pump with a handle that measured one gallon of gasoline for the occasional Model T, Gray Dort or Four 90 car.

My first chore when my aunt and uncle departed was to don a white apron and lean across the counter. I was the master of all I surveyed. Then I swung out the great barrels of oatmeal and sugar from under the counter and sampled them. A good half hour was spent examining the labels of the medicine bottles. It seemed as if everybody in our community had kidney and liver trouble from the bewildering array of pills and medicines on those few shelves.

Minnie Macpherson could be counted upon to call at least twice to see if the mailman had arrived. Occasionally a youngster came for coal oil, tea, sugar or tobacco for their elders. I always managed to put on a very impressive show for them. This was especially so when I had to look up the charge books in the rack under the counter, mark down the items and give them their bills. I felt, by knowing how much each family owed my uncle, almost as important as the royal treasurer, all the more so because of the stern lectures I had been given about never divulging the figures to my schoolmates.

The arrival of the mailman brought the newspaper and the occasional catalogue or magazine. I gave the mailman several emergency orders to deliver that had been telephoned in by people living on the concession. These were usually for an extra ball of binder twine, some bolts or machine oil. Although the government frowned on such delivery service it was considered to be almost the duty of the mailman, who at that time depended for his job more or less on the good will of the local Member of Parliament, and hence the good will of our community.

There was also an element of surprise in the whole affair. Searching for a carborundum stone, a file, cotter pins, a milk strainer, sticky fly-paper, formaldehyde, paraffin, neat's-foot oil, three-inch spikes, quarter-inch trip-rope, shoe laces, cream of tartar, size thirty jersey drawers, a yard and a quarter of fifty-four-inch white oilcloth or a box of soft-nosed .22 calibre bullets brought out the diversity and richness of the stock in the store.

A commercial traveller would sometimes come along. Finding my uncle away he would look over the stock of his own commodity, make up a list of what he thought the store needed and leave a copy, saying that he would call that night to confirm the order. Then he would treat me to a bottle of soda pop or a chocolate bar and rest for a time in the cool depths of the store and pass the time away in easy, friendly conversation.

From these "drummers" I acquired a red Whoopee cap which Mother wouldn't let me wear, a pearl-handled jack-knife which I lost down a well, a glass ball with a snowstorm concealed inside which reposed in our front parlour for many years, and several magazines with revealing pictures which were consumed by our kitchen stove after Father found them in the driving-shed.

I was paid meticulously by my uncle at the rate of twenty-five cents an hour. This was a sum of tremendous proportions in those days and helped to confirm in my mind the solemn ambition that someday I would be the proud proprietor of a country store. I didn't ponder on the mystery of how he was able to pay me this amount, since the commercial travellers were the only ones who paid cash, the other purchases being simply recorded in the mysterious books in the shelf under the counter.

The month-long holidays enjoyed by most present-day farms lead me to remember our annual vacation when I was a boy on the farm. It happened after seeding and before haying and usually when school was out. It always came about in an unexpected way, too. On a Friday morning Father announced, "I think we might take a little trip to the lake to-morrow." It was always planned for a Saturday. This gave it the air of being a holiday. In other words, it was a day of work which was being converted into one of leisure.

Mother would begin preparations even before the breakfast dishes had been done up. What a scene that kitchen was! There were cakes and pies to bake, a ham to boil, a chicken to roast and bread to be baked.

There was no question of how we children worked on that Friday. The woodbox swelled to overflowing. There was enough kindling split and stacked in the woodshed to last for a month. We amazed our elders by even washing out the milk pails and the milk tins. This was a job we managed to escape at least four times out of seven.

We were sent to bed early with the mistaken conviction that we needed extra rest. Try as we might, sleep just wouldn't come. It was delicious to lie awake and watch the old moon filtering through the pine trees outside the window, contemplating the possibilities of the next day.

Long before the first glimmer of the sun could be seen we were alert and waiting. Our ears were trained for that first sound of protest from the bed springs as Father swung from the bed and touched his feet to the floor. On other occasions we dawdled as long as possible but this was a morning when every moment counted.

It seemed such a long time until the chores were finished. Breakfast and the loading of the democrat or, later on, the Model T, took an interminable period of time. At last we were coasting along the road, and gradually the air of holiday took over the party. Even Father, at the sight of other people going to their barns to do chores, felt like the lucky man who can idle while others must work.

Father and Grandfather solemnly discussed the farms and the look of the fields and the fences. Mother and Aunt Millie who came along for the ride, the prerogative of a spinster, took notice of the wash lines, front lawns and flower beds. When these had been discussed to breaking point they launched into general gossip about their relatives.

To land-locked farm boys the sight of a harbour, a beach and the lake had all the charm a tourist finds in the first glimpse of Tahiti or Bali. Under the protective covering of blankets we managed to change to swim suits, an affectation which we managed to escape when we went swimming in the river.

The lake water on a warm day has the true levelling influence. Town kids and country kids played happily together unless the towners were sharp enough to notice the degree of tan of the country boys. After an exhausting number of hours in the water we were all called to a spot on the beach where the food was spread out by Mother. She had, in fact, spent almost all the time since our arrival fussing over it.

Back in the car, under the protective covering of the blankets, we reverted to our regular clothes. Grandfather was beginning to fidget. He always fidgeted under certain circumstances. Sometimes, by wandering over to the dock, he found a man of his own age to smoke and chat with. This kept him occupied only if the man wanted to talk crops and prices. It was unfortunate, however, that most of the older men he met were usually fishermen or retired businessmen. On these occasions he was always pushing to go home early.

We were usually given an hour to explore with the strict admonition to stay away from the ships and the harbour. Heading in the direction of town we usually ended up by the ships in the harbour. It was spectacular to watch the deck hands walking around nonchalantly, as the great spouts sucked grain from the bowels of the ships, while an old-timer on the ship tossed repartee at us.

We were always late getting back to the family. They sat waiting, all packed and full of scold. Scolding didn't do much good at a time like that, though; we were too full of the good feeling of the day and the treasure-house of memories. Father's anger lessened as we moved through the town with its first lights coming on in the stores. In town, Father stopped. Grandfather grumbled about the chores but Father pretended he didn't hear him. We got a glimpse of an ice-cream parlour with people sitting around inside and it was like getting a glimpse of a railroad diner as the train sped along through our valley. Father went in and came out a few minutes later with ice-cream cones for everyone. This made the day complete.

By the time we got home all the children were asleep, and even Mother was alternately dozing and fussing about somebody's falling out. When we arrived at the house Father said, "Well, we've had our holiday, so you children go to bed and Pa and I will do the chores." Then he added gruffly to

Mother, "And you go to bed, too, and don't be doing those dishes to-night."

Our dreams that night were filled with a strange conglomeration of the sights and sounds of the day—a day complete—the day of our annual vacation.

21
CHANGE AND PROGRESS

WITHOUT ARGUING ABOUT THE MERITS OF PROgress I can look back on some bygone things that are pleasant to remember, such as the periodic visits of the horse-trader.

During the early summer horse-traders used to wander up and down the concession looking for a "dicker." The horse-trader was always welcomed by the head of the household, for he carried with him a fair load of gossip about the community. If he didn't have any he could always manufacture enough for good conversation.

As a boy I can remember the horse-trader driving a fancy horse and rig, and smoking a cigar, shining with an air of prosperity like the enamel on his buggy. Later on the picture changed as horses became less important in the scheme of things in the country. I can remember one day when Mother looked out and saw a dejected horse pulling a sagging buggy in which sat a man who had a lead rope on three or four horses walking in file behind.

That was the signal for her to say, "Hmph, there'll be no work done around here to-day." My father was wise enough to keep quiet as she spluttered, "And I suppose that old goat will come in and eat his fool head off again." It wasn't that she begrudged the food, but she always had a fear of Father's getting the worst of a deal.

Father didn't say anything. He just lit his pipe, put on his hat and went outside. He talked to the trader for a while and after they had looked over the string of horses, they moved on down to the barn. Usually they spent the afternoon there. At supper-time Father brought him up to the house for a meal and Mother glared at both of them. However, the horse-trader started off by praising the biscuits and the meat, and threw out a little gossip. First thing I knew, Mother was talking to him as if he were the most welcome guest that had ever crossed the doorstep.

Horse-traders were shrewd men. They lived by their wits and their ability to judge horseflesh. Some were not above doing a little "doctoring" to give a horse a better appearance.

And they were good sports. At various times they were all nipped in a deal. Often it was a case of their selling a horse believing they couldn't get a worse one in trade, and ending up with a decrepit old nag that could hardly carry its own weight around; but they never bemoaned the deal. Usually they went back to get even.

Many stories have been told about horse-traders. One of the best concerns a certain sharp dealer who had doctored up a "heavy" horse. He appeared at a farmer's place with the horse all groomed up and shiny. The farmer looked the horse over carefully. "Do you like that coat?" inquired the trader. "Oh, the coat's all right," replied the farmer, "It's the pants I don't like."

Horse-traders knew everybody in the country. When the occasion arose to ship a carload of horses, they picked out the names of men who had horses to sell. They paid them honest prices and made a fair profit on the transaction. Their time between such sales was spent "gypsying." Ready and willing to do you a favour at any time, good talkers and well-travelled, they helped to break the monotony of farm life with their visits.

The horse-traders have vanished, although you find them occasionally, sitting around on hotel verandas in small country villages or at a grist mill or a livery stable that has been converted into a garage. They're old men now, living from pension cheque to pension cheque because it is a truism of the country that a "horse-trader never makes any money in the end."

Puffing on his pipe and squinting under white eyebrows, an old man may recognize you, but never by name. It will always be, "Oh yes, you're on the fourth concession. I traded a bay mare with your father in '22 for a gelding." Then he's off in a flood of reminiscences.

"I tell you, the day will come when men will be using horses again on the land. Tractor fumes are poisoning it. You'll find there'll be prosperity again."

There were other things in our community that were subject to change. They were somehow less personal than the horse-traders.

I was driving back in the wagon from the village with my father one early summer afternoon. He had had to break harvest because of the weather and had taken the opportunity to go in for grist. As we were coming down the concession big thunderheads assembled over the far hills of the valley. It looked like a storm and there were only two places where we could take shelter. It would have to be either the township hall or the big maple tree by Macphersons'.

We passed the hall and drove on as the first gusts of wind were stirring up licks of dust. The maples were showing the white undersides of their leaves, like maidens covering a set of blushing faces with white petticoats. The first big splattering drops of rain came down erratically. Father nudged the horses and we made it to the shelter of the enormous maple tree, just as the rain began to belt down.

It was always called "the tree at the jog." Actually, the roadmakers had considerately passed around the tree when it was first encountered by the township surveyors. It must have had a distinct character to have impressed them at that time. Part of its secret was a limb that came straight out and then shot up at a right angle. If it had been the Wild West there might have been reason for making it a "hanging tree."

That tree, just as on the day when we were caught by the rain, was a familiar landmark to all of us in the township. People posted bills on the big trunk, and made appointments to meet under it.

I can remember envying the bigger boys who used to climb into the leafy security of the tree and play highwaymen. My turn came, but a prank, when someone added the realistic touch of trying to lasso passing residents, backfired in an ugly way. Billy Deakin dropped a lasso, trying to catch the large ornamented hat of one of the Jenkins spinsters, but the rope dropped around her shoulders, half dragging her out of the buggy and pulling Billy onto the road. The tree was forthwith declared forbidden territory by my parents as well as the teacher, who happened that year to be a strong-willed specimen of womanhood.

On the day we stopped to wait out the storm under the great, spreading arms of "the tree at the jog," my father lit his pipe. It was comfortable under the leafy seclusion of its branches, with the rain spattering down outside and an occasional vagrant drop trickling through.

"It's a wonderful tree," I remarked.

My father took the pipe from his mouth and nodded.

"That tree is something of a symbol in our locality. My boy, the first men who came to this valley were like that tree. Take those old men you see in town. Most of them are retired now but they're big, broad-shouldered men. Some of them started their own farms here. Old Sandy Jack Macpherson cleared his own farm. Those men stand straight and tall in spite of their years and they sort of spread out. They took roots in this soil and they spread their arms out over the land and those arms are like their families. It will be a sorry day for all of us when they pass on."

I said, "But the tree will still be here."

Father said in a quiet voice, "Let us hope so, my boy. Let us hope so."

Then something happened that seemed a prophetic answer to our hopes and fears for the tree. There was a meeting of the township council that almost developed into violence. The reeve and one of the councillors wanted to cut down the old maple tree so that the road could be straightened. Letters were written to the local newspaper. The editor stood for the tree. Neighbours argued and talked incessantly. The reeve was voted out at the next election. The man who was next elected reeve learned from his predecessor's mistake and shelved the matter of the tree's being cut down.

The controversy flared up from time to time but it seemed as if no one really wanted to get involved in it. I was going to high school when somebody noticed that the old tree was sick. The older folks blamed it on the gasoline fumes from passing cars. Others said it was a blight. The centre of the tree seemed to be drying up because the leaves turned brown and dead in midsummer.

The tree didn't respond next spring. In late summer when it was time for road work, the tree was cut down.

After that there was a sad gap in the road as we drove into the village. We noticed it in the way one notices the absence of a friend who has passed on. But slowly I forgot the tree, except sometimes when I read the obituary notices in the weekly paper and remembered what Father had said.

When the last of the Macphersons had left the land a stranger bought the farm. He soon built a new house to replace the log one that had been retained for so many years with an artificial coating of stucco. Nowadays I sometimes remember the tree and when I do, I remember old Sandy Jack Macpherson.

22
THE BAREFOOT DAYS

HOW WE YEARNED FOR THE TIME WHEN SHOES and stockings could be shucked in the early summer! There has been a deplorable tendency of late to rob children of this great privilege.

Why is it that recently so many of us have all but forgotten the pleasures we had as children in bare feet? I remember how anxiously I waited for that first sunny day when Mother could be convinced that it was warm enough for barefoot romping. Of course we didn't admit it, but we had already been peeling off our shoes and stockings on the way to school, as soon as we rounded the curve that took us out of the vision of the kitchen windows.

How thrilling it was to walk on the gravel with winter-tender feet! How the pebbles itched in the instep and nipped around the toes! For those first few times we had to walk on the beaten track of the road and hope ardently that no new gravel had been applied on the roadway. But tender feet soon vanished after a few days of travelling on the gravel roads of the township.

I remember the adventure of a stubble field. It took careful navigating to escape the thistles and the stubble. Another source of pleasure was dipping my feet in the creek while sitting on the old culvert. The water was warm and the creek meandered along, seemingly in no hurry to reach the river.

When I pulled my feet out there would be a collection of bloodsuckers hanging on for dear life. City children were always afraid of the little black creatures, but there wasn't a country lad who hadn't heard that old superstition about their being healthy because they were supposed to cleanse your blood.

City children may take off their shoes and stockings on occasion, to splash in the water of a hose. They probably enjoy it, too. It has always been the heritage of the country children, however, to doff their shoes and stockings in early spring. They progress, barefoot, through the summer and fall until their mothers finally lay down the law and insist upon their wearing them again.

We hated to wash our feet. Mother came up and, in place of tucking us in, she flipped the covers off our feet. Woe betide the one caught slipping between the sheets without washing. I remember how I would scrub in a half-hearted way at my feet, only to have Mother's scrutiny call my attention to rings of dirt around the calf of my leg. Punishment was also meted out on several occasions to a certain boy who, instead of securing the wash basin and filling it with water, dipped his feet in the rain barrel at the corner of the kitchen, hoping in this way to escape.

When our feet had really toughened up, we were able to walk in hay stubble. However, haying, like the barefoot days, has changed. They put hay up in rolls and square bundles now, and much of the fun has been taken out of the operation. Mind you, they've eliminated a lot of the work as well, but there was a pleasant atmosphere to haying that has vanished with the advent of so many mechanical aids.

There was, first of all, the steady "clackety-clack" of the

mower as the horses plodded along and knife blades see-sawed through aromatic clover or timothy. The small inhabitants of the paths in the forest of hay scampered out in mortal fright. Here and there a rabbit would go "lipperty-lipping" out of danger and there was an occasional stop to remove a bird's nest to the safety of the fence bottom.

A hayfield had an aroma that was distinctive. The poets have written countless lines about the smell of new-mown hay. There wasn't time for poetic thoughts in a hayfield, but I was always aware of a sense of satisfaction as the straight swath came out neatly behind the cutting bar of the mower.

That same feeling came as I stopped with the horses under a shady tree, took a drink of crystal clear spring water from the bubbling pipe by the trough in the pasture, and then went back to sprawl for a rest against the fence, while the horses switched lazily and feasted on the delicate tops of the hay within their reach.

Raking hay was a job of an entirely different sort. Here I had to have my wits about me as the rake scooped up the swaths of hay and I dumped each rakeful into what I hoped would be neat windrows. The neater the windrow, the easier it was to coil.

There was a knack to coiling hay. Some men tugged and pulled and shoved and erected ugly-looking lumps in the field. My grandfather prided himself on the expert way he could coil hay. He had a flick of the wrist that seemed to pluck just the right amount of hay from the windrow. Finally, a larger forkful would be added that covered up the whole affair. The finished product looked like an old-fashioned beehive, covered with thatch.

The proof of the coil came when it was forked onto the wagon. The poor coil was an effort to handle. It tumbled apart, and was probably mouldy if there had been any recent rainfall. A good coil fitted neatly into three forkfuls, making it easier for the man on the load to place it.

Riding the wagon back to the barn came as a welcome respite. It was sheer pleasure to sprawl amid the sweet-smelling hay as the wagon lurched in the ruts like a galleon on a heavy sea.

Sometimes I sprang a short plank or scantling into the back of the wagon box under the hayrack, plunged my fork into the load, and then had a most precarious ride back to the barn.

The difficulty, of course, was that when riding in such a position I was expected to open and close all the gates on the way to and from the barn.

Sometimes, when driving a load of hay, it was difficult to gauge the side of the roadway. More than one load has been spilled over the edge of a culvert or the side of the gangway because of a miscalculation. That was when haying really seemed to be work. A second handling seemed to be such a waste of time and effort.

Our one concession to mechanical means came at the barn. The wagon was driven on to the barn floor, where the team was unhitched and taken outside for the task of pulling the hay-rope.

The hay-fork was plunged deep into the load, cocked so as to bite into the hay. The team was driven down the gangway and one man was stationed with the trip-rope. The bundle went swiftly to the roof of the barn, rolling along the track. Then as the trip-rope was pulled, the bundle plunged into the mow and the fork was pulled back for another bundle. "Mowing" the hay meant spreading the bundle out evenly and tramping it, while the team and wagon and men returned to the field for another load.

There was always the danger of fire from spontaneous combustion in the haying season. It could be caused by heated hay or grain, usually attributed to dampness. Sometimes a man was tempted to take a chance on semi-cured hay or grain and put it in the mow because of haste or the fear of a wet spell. But the peril remained even when a farmer took the best of precautions and dried the hay thoroughly before mowing it.

Barefoot days and haying time bring back many pleasant memories. One year, for instance, the hay was dry before it was cut and we all had to work very hard and for long hours to get it all in before the weather broke. At supper-time on an evening when we were worn out from working in the blazing sun, we came back to the house to find that Mother had set up our supper in the orchard. Just where the break in the trees caught the first whispers of evening breeze, she had arranged sawhorses with a storm door laid across them. It was covered with a tablecloth on which a delicious-looking supper of potato salad and cold chicken was spread out.

Suddenly our tiredness seemed to vanish. Father, never given to long speeches, came over from washing up and stood looking at the table:

"Well now, doesn't that beat all."

That little variation in the routine of living seemed to give everybody fresh energy. The empty dishes and dirty plates were taken to the house and we all went back to work in the fields. The sudden spurt of energy brought all the cured hay to the barn and the last wagon load was left in the gathering darkness on the barn floor. That night after midnight, the first few splatters of rain came blobbing down and it poured for over an hour. Lying in the darkness I could imagine that everyone was being thankful in his own way. Mother, I imagined, was smiling, thinking that perhaps the orchard supper had been a help in our never-ending battle with nature and the elements.

Cars were still a novelty in our community. There were quite a number of them around but they were mostly Model T's or Four 90's. Occasionally, a livestock buyer had a Durant or a Star. Most of them were dull black and boxy-looking touring cars with flapping side curtains for protection against the weather.

During a particularly hot election campaign the help of a cabinet minister had been enlisted on behalf of the local candidate. This naturally caused a flurry in the community. He was staying at the hotel in town. He had a very big car and a chauffeur, as well as a male secretary. The local switchboard operator in the municipal telephone company had started putting on airs because of the number of long distance telephone calls she was making.

"When I was talking to the Ottawa operator. . . ." was beginning to be her normal opening words for every speech.

In the unruffled calm of our community, the coming of the cabinet minister made conversation. I hadn't thought very much about either the politicians or the car, until one hot day when I was reading a book in the shade of the big, old pine tree, a tremendous black car came nosing in the front laneway. There was a man in the front seat and two men in the back. One of them got out and I saw it was the local member. He asked for my father and I merely pointed to the barn and stared in bug-eyed wonder at the car.

The man in the back seat beckoned to me. I somewhat reluctantly edged toward the car.

"Like this car?" asked an affable man with greying hair.

I muttered something.

"Like to go for a ride?"

This was too much for even an answer. I nodded.

"Run and tell your mother that you're coming with me."

My mother wouldn't believe me but came to the kitchen door rubbing her hands on her apron.

"It's all right," assured the man in the back, "I thought he might like a ride in this car."

He smiled, and said, "He seems to like it."

Mother vainly tried to get me inside for a wash and a change of clothes but I was too quick for her. The gentleman lifted his hat to her, tapped on the glass that divided him from the front seat where the driver was sitting and we drove out the laneway and down the road.

There I was, clothed only in dirt and a pair of overalls, sitting on the plush seats with my dirty bare feet sticking out.

"How do you like it?" enquired my benefactor as he lit a cigar and gravely handed me the paper ring from it.

I couldn't do justice to a description of that ride. The man had been raised in a remote area of northern Ontario. He certainly seemed to know what boys liked, because we stopped at the corner store and he sent the chauffeur in for a big bag of candy. Then I was handed a speaking tube. He solemnly asked me to tell the chauffeur to turn around and drive home.

Long after the car had gone I sat, not even eating the candy, and pondered on the wonderment of the afternoon. I can also say truthfully, that even now, long after the death of that political gentleman, I cannot tolerate a word of criticism about the Honourable Peter Heenan.

I don't know how he was about voters, but he certainly knew the way to a barefoot boy's heart.

23

PAYING THE MORTGAGE

THERE ISN'T MUCH USE TRYING TO HOLD BACK progress. It was flowing in, even when I was a boy. My father made me realize that no matter how self-contained you were on your farm, you couldn't get away from new influences.

I suppose the rudest awakening came when Father went to pay his mortgage one year.

Our mortgage came due on March 15 and it was held by John Graham, a retired banker who lived in the village. Father never liked the idea of its coming due at that time of year when cash was often hard to come by, but John had always said, "Just pay me when you can. One of these days we'll switch it over to a more convenient month for you."

The result of this friendly business relationship was that he put off paying the mortgage each year until the beginning of June. John died just after he had paid the interest the previous year. Father had paid with three bags of potatoes from the pit, a load of maple and beech blocks and the remainder in cash.

The John Graham estate was being handled by a trust company in the city, or a trust and loan company, or whatever you call them. As far as Father could figure out, there wasn't much trust about the outfit. He was notified that a payment was due on March 15. He didn't have the cash because the pigs he had planned to sell weren't ready. Mother nudged him a few times about it but for some reason or other he didn't pay any attention to it.

M-Day arrived and flitted off into the past without anything happening. There arrived in the mail the following week, a firm but restrained letter. Father had obviously misplaced the notice or else it hadn't arrived. Would he please pay the mortgage interest?

"Those pigs will be fit to go in a couple of weeks," he said tossing the letter on the sideboard in the kitchen, "And I'll pay the mortgage then."

From then on it became a sort of comedy of errors. The pigs seemed to go back and they weren't ready to go as soon as he expected. Then he got a real hell-raiser from the mortgage firm, signed by A. L. Anderson. If A. L. Anderson had been around at that moment, Father would have poked him in the snout, having just spent two hours in a pigpen trying to chase the most stubborn pigs in the world up into Jennings' truck.

By the following week, however, Father had cooled off. After all, this fellow Anderson was only doing his job. He was probably a pretty likable fellow. He thought we might go to the city and pay the interest while Mother did a little shopping. There was also a breed meeting he wanted to attend.

Mother was overjoyed at the idea.

"I think I'll take along a bag of potatoes," he said in the early morning as we were getting ready to leave.

"Oh, don't be silly," Mother laughed, "That Mr. Anderson wouldn't even appreciate potatoes."

Father couldn't quite see that. These were good pit potatoes and any city people Father ever met always seemed to appreciate them. He took a bag of them out of the root cellar and put them in the back of the car, taking care to wrap the bag in a horse blanket so they wouldn't bruise.

When the first novelty of driving had worn off I started to doze. Funny thoughts, dreams and ideas came tumbling into my mind. I must confess I was thinking a lot about the ritual of paying the mortgage.

I was quite a small boy the first time my grandfather had allowed me to accompany him on this important mission. He talked about it for several days. Then, one night, he announced in a grave voice that the occasion had arrived.

"Will you boys put a load of those maple blocks on the wagon. Take the ones from the far pile. I'll take that side of pork and two bags of potatoes. I'm going in to see Ike Smith."

Having delivered this announcement he leaned back in his chair as if to weigh the effect it had on his audience. There was silence. My father looked at me and then turned to where Grandfather sat at the head of the table.

"Harry's anxious to go."

Grandfather stroked his beard and looked at me. I was ready to slide under the table.

"He can come."

My heart seemed to explode in that instant.

"I'll give you a couple of jars of preserves for Mrs. Smith, William," said my grandmother as she got up from the table, "I know she's very fond of that wild strawberry jam."

We started out the next morning on the wagon. It was a long and jolting journey but a most enjoyable one. Grandfather was in good humour. This was evidenced by his desire to sing a long and rather rambling song, which he delivered in a high-pitched voice with absolutely no sense of melody.

Isaac Smith lived in a great Victorian house with a gingerbread fringe running along the edge of a veranda which covered three sides of the house. There was a driveway up to the front of the house which sat quite a long way from the street. The lawn had a freshly clipped look about it and there were plenty of flowering bushes and shrubs.

To me, it was a palace. I had seen such places from a distance, but on the auspicious occasion of paying the interest on the mortgage I might even get to see the inside of this one. I was already gloating over the stories I could tell at school.

Mr. Smith had a white goatee and a shock of silvery hair. He was wearing a smoking jacket and a pair of carpet slippers. I noticed that there was a very sharp press to his pants and that he had a black string tie around the stiffly starched collar on his shirt. He reminded me of pictures I had seen in books in the school library.

Mr. Smith called for an individual by the name of Pete. He was a slow-moving fellow, later identified as the handyman. He took the team and drove around beside the house.

We were shown into a room lined with books in glass cases. It was a wonderful place, with comfortable wicker chairs and a leather couch. On the floor were two bearskins. The place was saturated with the smell of tobacco smoke.

I sat with my cap in my hand while a pleasant half-hour of banter and conversation took place between my grandfather and Mr. Smith. When they talked about politics I was lost. I took more interest when they talked about the weather. Then, the conversation took a new direction.

I gathered, and was feeling very sorry about it, that this was an exceedingly bad time for anybody who had money out on loan. My grandfather seemed to be sympathetic and he then told Mr. Smith how poor the crops had been and went into great detail about the heifer that had just freshened and then bloated and died on the spring grass. I was confused because Grandfather had been boasting to almost everyone about how good his crops had been.

They sparred back and forth. My grandfather was, I discovered, quite adroit at talking to the distinguished-looking money-lender. Mr. Smith, too, had his tricks. When he was being cornered in the conversation he would turn and ask me how old I was, and what book I was in at school. He asked me the same question three times!

Finally, when I was beginning to wonder if they would ever get around to the subject of the mortgage, it came up in conversation. Mr. Smith was almost apologetic for having sent the notice. My grandfather ignored that and changed the subject. He pointed out how hard it was to get good dry hard wood for burning in a heater and how the price for wood was certainly going to go up. Mr. Smith nodded. Then Grandfather started telling about the complaints of some of his neighbours that their potatoes had a sort of blight on them. Mr. Smith filled his pipe and nodded once or twice.

Mr. Smith, who seemed not to have noticed that we had arrived with a load of wood and some potatoes, asked my grandfather if he had any wood to sell. That worthy bluffer then said he had half-promised a load to John Donnelley, the hardware merchant.

Mr. Smith opened a small cabinet and took out a bottle and two glasses.

"Sorry, you can't join us, son," he smiled, "But your grandfather will have your share."

Mrs. Smith appeared and spoke to us. She was a kind-faced woman with white hair. She went away and came back with a glass of lemonade and a plate of cookies. Neither Mr. Smith nor my grandfather touched the cookies on the plate but I managed several.

Grandfather finally suggested that if Mr. Smith really needed wood, he might be able to spare him a jag. Mr. Smith said that this was very kind and they haggled in a good-natured way about the price.

"You couldn't see your way clear to letting me have a few potatoes, could you, William?" he asked.

My grandfather swallowed deeply from the glass and stroked his beard.

"Well, I know how hard they're going to be to get later on in the fall. I guess I could let you have two bags."

Mr. Smith then fixed a pair of glasses on his nose in a position which I thought was precarious and began to figure with a pen on a long sheet of paper. Grandfather watched over his shoulder. Finally, after a great deal of calculation, a figure was struck. Grandfather took out a deep, leather purse and paid the balance in cash. Mr. Smith then gave Grandfather a cigar and they shook hands.

I was sent out to tell Peter to unload the wood and potatoes. I brought back the two jars of wild strawberry jam and gave them to Mrs. Smith who was sitting with her knitting in what I guessed was the parlour. She looked very pleased and ushered me back to the dining-room where there was a glass of milk and some sandwiches. Hunger drove away my shyness, although the portraits on the walls of the fierce-looking men and women disconcerted me a little.

Mrs. Smith gave me a bundle and a stick of licorice candy. She told me that the bundle contained a dress for my mother to make over and a jar of mustard pickles for my grandmother.

Just before leaving, my grandfather remembered, seemingly just in the nick of time, that he had a cured ham. This he proceeded to give to Mr. Smith, who beamed with pleasure. Mr. Smith then asked Grandfather to come back into the house for a brief visit. I was left holding the team. Grandfather came out a half hour later wiping his moustache. He sang on the way home and we stopped by the river to eat the lunch which Mrs. Smith had pressed on him, after he had refused to stay for dinner.

The team were eating the hay in the wagon box and we had cold spring water to drink with the sandwiches. Grandfather lay back in the grass. He presented quite a startling figure, as the sunlight slanting through the trees caught and was reflected on his golden-red whiskers. He looked like a creature from another world.

"M'lad," he said, "That's the way to do business. Ike Smith is a gentleman."

My father had dealt with John Graham in the same way when he took over the farm from Grandfather. John, who had been the local bank manager, had also been a great lacrosse player, and had tutored Father in the game. The mortgage was never a source of embarrassment to either of them. If Father were late in paying the mortgage he simply added something he knew John would like.

Driving to the city to see A. L. Anderson, I couldn't help thinking of those rather comfortable arrangements.

Shortly after ten in the morning we arrived in the city. Mother was in mortal terror but Father grasped the wheel with full determination. I gazed unafraid out of the window, fascinated by the bustle of city traffic.

There was a good deal of confusion in the matter of finding the headquarters of the trust company. Father, on the scanty knowledge of two previous visits to the city, was determined to find the place without asking directions. Mother's sudden headache drove him to ask a policeman. We had stopped in front of the proper building but had to drive to another place, because there was no parking on that side of the street. Then it took a half hour of searching to walk back and find the trust company building.

Mother was taking no chances. She took a taxi to Eaton's. I was allowed to go with Father but was told I might have to wait if A. L. Anderson wanted to get acquainted over a friendly drink. Father was figuring on establishing a friendly contact with the trust company official.

The company was established in what might have been a Greek temple at one time. It wasn't at all what I had expected. The lobby was big enough to hold a hundred loads of cured hay.

Father moved around from place to place. Every person he asked just pushed him on to the next one. Finally, a rather pleasant woman who took pity on his plight, told him to go to the Mortgage Department on the second floor.

A. L. Anderson turned out to be a brisk-looking woman with hair that must have been dyed red, but had come out a sort of purple colour. She wore funny-shaped glasses, behind which lurked green eyes. All in all, she looked like some new type of cat.

She looked Father over coolly, flipped a filing thing around and picked up a card. Then she made him feel like a criminal as she reminded him that the interest was many days overdue. She quickly figured out how much extra there was to pay. Father handed over the money. She thanked him in a voice that would keep ice-cream hard on a July day and turned away from the counter.

Some strange impulse made Father ask, "Do you like pit potatoes?"

She turned and replied disdainfully, "I can't eat potatoes. They're fattening."

Father talked for an hour after we left the city, but lapsed into sullen silence when Mother enquired, "Didn't A. L. Anderson invite you out for a friendly drink?" If I hadn't known before about the world's changing, I certainly knew about it after that trip.

24

DIFFICULT WEATHER DAYS

PROBABLY THE MOST DIFFICULT TIME OF A BOY'S life in the country came in the early summer. Outside the walls of the schoolhouse there was a green world of growing things and the sort of activity that every youth enjoyed. Inside, there was the daily regimentation of classes and lessons. The end of the school term seemed to be an eternity away.

Looking back on it, I am sure it wasn't any fun for the teacher either. A large part of the attendance was made up of older boys who started school late in the fall, spent most of the winter there, left for the seeding and straggled back in when they felt like it until the end of the term.

Between the teacher and the older boys there was an armed truce. She had the authority of the schoolboard to back her up, as well as a fear that it might not act if she did have to appeal to it. The big boys, blustering and full of bravado, had a semi-respect for her authority. They also had a healthy respect for what their parents might do if they challenged the teacher.

"Red Lead" Mullin was a character. A big, lanky boy of seventeen, he had once almost poisoned himself by consuming red lead on a dare, and had had to be pumped out by Doctor Macdonald. The name stuck with him. Powerful and yet strangely gentle with the younger children, he wasn't challenged by any of our older pupils after he had tossed a local giant by the name of "Samson" Macgillvray into the creek without much effort.

"Red Lead" went to school because he wanted to read. He paid little or no attention to classes but sat in his seat and devoured all the books he could get his hands on. I suppose he went through the small, school library at least four times and had on call an amazing amount of information on everything from bee-keeping to love sonnets.

Our teacher at that time was Marie Fogg. She was diminutive, with a small face adorned by a prominent nose and a mass of red hair. She terrified all of us and even induced fear in the seasonal students, but "Red Lead" paid no attention to her. He roused himself sufficiently at Christmas-time to give a recitation at the concert. About this time he even made one or two wrong answers in arithmetic, but by the time of the Valentine Box Social he had gone back to reading.

One fine day towards the end of the school year when the outside world was particularly appealing, the atmosphere in the schoolhouse was charged with tension. When two small girls upset the water pail, Miss Fogg let loose for a terrible minute or two, and then recovered her poise. She didn't recover in time, however, to prevent a youth and a rapidly maturing young girl from seizing the water pail and heading for the church pump, a quarter of a mile away.

We were all given work then, which I suppose she hoped would keep us occupied. It didn't. She paced back and forth and peeked out of the windows and wrote on the blackboard and then erased her own words. The incident was a welcome diversion for all of us.

Once or twice Miss Fogg seemed on the point of sending someone after the pair. She would stop in her pacing, start to speak and then mutter something about all of us keeping on with our work. She was in what my grandfather would have called a "real tizzy."

It was just before recess time when the girl re-appeared. Her hair was mussed and she was holding a tear in her dress with one hand. She seemed to have been running and her cheeks were flushed and red. The youth had a scratch on his cheek and a smirk on his face.

"What happened?" demanded Miss Fogg.

Silence. We all came fully alive. "Red Lead" emerged from his *History of The Great War.* The pair stood silently.

"I asked you a question."

The girl mumbled something about running and falling. The boy shuffled his feet and Miss Fogg made a grab for the hame-strap which was hanging on the side of her desk. We gasped. Strapping was a common enough thing for boys but we had never seen a girl strapped.

"Hold out your hands. Imagine the pair of you. Common tramps, that's what you are."

"Red-Lead" ambled down the aisle, stepped between the boy and girl and faced the teacher.

"Miss Fogg, you ain't going to strap a girl!"

He didn't put it in the form of a question. It was a statement and Miss Fogg lashed out at him blindly with the strap. This was excitement of the highest form. I thought I was going to explode when the big lad reached out calmly and took the strap away from her. When she struggled, he simply picked her up and stood her on the desk.

"Cool off," he said, and as she started to move from the desk, he gently pushed her back. "Be good now, Miss Fogg, or I'll cool you off with that pail of water."

Well, our school hero proceeded to send the boy and girl home, dismiss all of us for recess and then lift the struggling Miss Fogg from the desk. We huddled outside in groups and wondered about the whole affair in a kind of awed respect. Even the older boys who used to delight in teasing the smaller children were strangely silent.

"Red Lead" stayed on reading his book, even after recess. Miss Fogg just sat at her desk and let all of us read, dismissing us at three thirty instead of four o'clock.

Next day our hero didn't appear at school. The matter was never discussed in school again. It was talked about at great length in the community and helped to make the days pass much more quickly until the closing of school.

Miss Fogg didn't come back the next year. We had a man who brooked no interruptions in his classroom, but I do think that when the warm days of early summer came along, even he was tempted to moon at the windows.

Ever since I was a boy on the farm, talking about weather has been a comfort and privilege that almost everybody indulges in.

I can remember hearing my grandfather in bed at night groaning as he turned, and in the morning he would say to Mother, "Better get the youngsters to wear slickers, it's going to rain before night." Sure enough it would rain, and I grew to know that when he had the "neureetis," as he called it, it was a certain sign of rain.

It was the same way with my father. He had bunions that could give a twenty-four-hour prediction on a thunderstorm.

Weather was the bread and butter of conversation. When two women called on the party line, it was inevitable that they began by saying, "Isn't it hot to-day?" You couldn't hear the other side of the conversation but she probably replied, "Not as bad as yesterday, though," or else, "Dear me, and I thought yesterday was a bad one."

Weather was a godsend to horse-traders. They always approached each other like two veteran roosters, with mutual healthy respect. They wanted to test and sound so as not to be caught at a disadvantage. They could bring up the weather and chew it over well, before shifting gradually into the matter of concern.

Talking about the weather was a handy tool for barbers or general merchants, too. They met dozens of people in a day and it was always considered fair to have a romp about the weather before getting into local affairs.

Intellectuals may be able to meet and start right off about the matter in hand, but that doesn't apply to the boys waiting for grist at the mill. There's only so much local matter to chew on during a waiting session there, so they start off with a round about the weather and save the juicier morsels for later on, when the waiting gets a little harder or the bench wears closer to the bone.

We all grew up with our own sense of weather forecasting. Some people knew it would rain when the leaves turned their white sides up. Nearly everyone had an ache, pain or twinge of some kind that, for them, had almost magical qualities. In town there were people who would bet you money when the sign in front of the drugstore made a strange "swhinggig" sound as it rocked in the breeze. Others placed their bets on the sounds of the trains. They were certain when you could hear the sound of the "dayliner" in the valley next to ours that we were in for what they called a "soft" spell. Of course, the bets were never paid because everybody understood the spirit of the thing.

Every time the minister grew tired of repeating sermons even he fell back on the topic: "This blessed weather which we will have for our harvest comes from the hands of Providence." Sometimes in the spring he threw in a lick before seeding. When rain was approaching after a dry, hot spell in the summer-time, he hit a real bonanza.

Weather gave cousins who hated each other a wonderful chance, when they met in the post office or the general store, to give the lie in public to the tradition of their enmity. They had a gabfest of predictions about the weather possibilities for the coming social events and passed the meeting off in a lady-like fashion.

The older folks who sat on the veranda of the hotel in the summer-time and the lobby of the post office in the winter-time had been hashing the weather over for years. They specialized in remembering when the "big storm" of such and such a year happened. It might also be said that they specialized in trying to disprove each other. If one said the biggest storm was in 1898 he was certain to be challenged by another who would say that it was 1900. Then the battle lines were formed. Evidence would be brought forward that the champion storm was in 1898, because that was the year the livery stable burned down. Contrasting evidence said it was 1900 because that was the year that Ed Hamilton went out West. So the battle raged, and when it came time to go home for supper everybody was pleased and nothing had been proven.

There were some people in our township who kept calendars marked for years with reports on the daily weather. In fact, Peter Fitzgerald got trapped that way. He was an inveterate bachelor who had been "going" with Martha

Simpson for some twenty-two years when she got fed up with feeding him and getting little but conversation out of it.

Martha faced Peter and told him she wanted to get married or else. Cannily he looked up his calendar record and saw that January 10 had been stormy for six years. He promised to marry her on January 10 if it were a fine day. It was one of the finest of the winter. Peter had overlooked the seven-year cycle of weather.

25

COUNTRY CUSTOMS

THE RAPID CHANGES IN RURAL LIVING CONstantly amaze me. Farmers to-day have all the modern conveniences of city living; a far cry from my boyhood days, when city people often thought us rather primitive. A few older farmers have stubbornly resisted the inroads made by modernization. They cling to their old way of life, and I for one am glad that they do, because it adds colour to the pattern of country living.

City people visiting the farm used to spend a great deal of time in speculation about how we managed to keep clean. In fact, I would not be at all surprised if some some of them were of the opinion that we allowed the dust to cake on and then peeled it off when it got too thick.

For some unknown reason the old log house, built by

Great-grandfather on the homestead, had been retained. It served variously as a woodshed and a storehouse for everything in general.

During the summer-time Father patronized it each Saturday night in order to take a bath. How well I can remember him standing in the washtub while one of the boys, sitting with the sprinkling can on a cross beam, gave him a shower. It was a hard job to carry the water, but the sprinkling was fun. The general rule was to give him one pailful for the front, another for the back and a third one for a general rub-down. The harvest dust melted before the spray from that old sprinkling can.

I can remember one time when a dose of Paris green had been placed in that can. I was doing the sprinkling that night. It was late evening and the light was dim up in the old house. I poured the pail of water into the can and proceeded to spray. Father stood there enjoying the trickling comfort of the water down his back when he realized that something was amiss. He was turning an alarming colour of green.

He pranced out of the tub and over to the light. Great-aunt Agatha was staying with us that week and when she caught a glimpse of a greenish figure dashing up to the doorway of the old shed, she screamed and fainted. What made Father really mad was her statement when she recovered. "I just saw that hideous thing that looked like a big bullfrog jumping around in there and I couldn't stand the sight."

We boys never had much use for the improvised bathing of the old log house. It was always a great deal more pleasant to go back to the swimming-hole in the river and enjoy unhampered bathing. But Saturday night was always bath night. Right after supper in the winter-time Mother placed the two boilers filled with water on top of the stove. By bedtime the boilers were sizzling and the lids jumping. The washtub was placed in the centre of the kitchen floor and the lamp set up on the sideboard so that no water could splash in the hot chimney. The women-folk then withdrew to the front parlour and the men began their bathing.

By common agreement one boiler of hot water was used by the men, the other by the women. The hot water was then rationed out, according to the number of men present. Bathing was always more fun when Father went straight to bed after his bath. A wet towel makes an excellent weapon for either defence or offence. Sometimes, when the playing got too rough and the water began to splash on the wallpaper, Mother sounded a warning rap on the kitchen door and the fun was over.

After the men-folk were away off to bed the women took their baths. At Sunday morning breakfast table Mother always commented on the confusion of clothes left behind. Shirts, socks, pants, towels, clothes of every description were apt to be found in all manner of places around the kitchen.

The Saturday night bath ritual changed a great deal with the advent of modern plumbing. Uncle Ab installed a new bathroom with all kinds of trimmings. Uncle Ab was a cattle buyer and although he complained all the time that he was not making money, he still managed to get it from somewhere. One reason he gave for the new bathroom was that when he made trips to the city he was constantly worried about how to use all the new gadgets which they were installing in hotel bathrooms.

On the other hand, I have an uncle who never was in favour of a fancy bathroom. When his wife had a sizeable amount of money left to her she remodelled the house and installed a new bathroom. My uncle was definitely "agin" it. He looked in after it was completed, spat his wad of tobacco into the wash basin in a thoughtful way and decided to stick to bathing in the driving-shed. He still does.

One thing that doesn't change, however, is the rural attitude to the common cold. Country people refuse to allow their colds to be deterred by such designations as "virus" or the use of a wide range of antibiotics.

This is more or less hereditary. I remember a hired man we had who was particularly susceptible to colds. Unlike the majority of us who succumbed to colds in damp, cold or wet weather, he managed to contract one in the middle of summer.

It started with a cough in the night. The minor barking developed into wholesale whooping that woke up the entire family. He arrived at the breakfast table looking like the remnant of a bad night.

"You look like something the cat dragged home," was the comment from Grandfather.

The hired man looked at Mother like a drowning spaniel

and said pleadingly, "Nothing for breakfast except a plate of onions with salt and vinegar."

He explained that this strange diet was a remedy used with success by his mother. Then he manfully attacked the mound of onions on his plate. We kept edging farther and farther away from him. Finally he gasped for breath and began to gulp water.

The only benefit that resulted from the onions was to keep us away from him. Then he remembered another cure. He crossed a pair of woollen stockings on his chest, next to his skin. I never knew whether this was for warmth or a sort of superstition. His cold grew steadily worse.

Next day he soaked his feet in a solution of mustard, salt and boiling water. Then he drank the juice of six roasted lemons without sugar in it. With his mouth puckered up like a frozen squash he tottered off to bed. At three the next morning he was up rustling through the pantry looking for baking soda which he intended mixing with hot milk and drinking.

When Mother mentioned on the party line that the hired man was sick, the cold cures started in earnest. Mrs. Wilson called to suggest that he pickle two duck livers in vinegar and salt overnight and eat them the next morning. Jake Harris suggested that he rub a mixture of axle grease and turpentine on his chest before going to bed. Joe Mallough sent a little sack over for him to wear around his neck. After a couple of days there was an unpleasant odour in the house. Mother finally demanded an investigation into the mysterious sack. It turned out that there was a pig's ear inside. Of course, the hired man couldn't smell it anyhow. Miss Simpson who lived in the village sent him out a teaspoonful of brandy. This, to the hired man who had a great capacity for any form of spirits, was like spitting in the Atlantic and expecting the tide to come in.

There were two sides to human nature where a cold was concerned. The first kind of people recounted to the hired man in great detail the time their Uncle Jim or their Cousin Millie took cold. There was a dramatic pause and then, "Poor soul didn't last long." Or else they would say, "Never was the same after that cold. Just couldn't shake it from the system, I guess."

That poor hired man heard the horrible details of more

deaths than could be found in a daily paper. Each one, it appeared, stemmed directly from a bad cold or a chill.

The second kind of visitor I noticed got right in the swim with cold cures. Some recommended drinking water and others said with a grave shake of the head, "Water's the worst thing you can take." Onion juice and liniment mixed with sugar seemed to be the most popular treatment. Rhubarb juice and chewing tobacco stewed together and taken by the spoonful was one party's contribution.

When the well-stocked shelves of the village drugstore were added to the home remedies, the country person had a formidable array of medicines with which to dose the old-fashioned cold. If deaths resulted, the "cold cures" were to blame, and not the illness.

26

SUMMER TRAVEL

MODERN FOLK DON'T APPRECIATE HOW MANY conveniences the passing of the years has brought them. Take, for instance, the simple process of going away. To-day, it's a matter of forgetting about the work there is to be done (which I find quite easy to do), stepping into the car and zipping along to where you happen to be going.

But back in the days when I was a boy, it was as complex as a large-scale military manœuvre. For quite some time Mother planned the trip over to Grandmother's place—a matter of eight miles. She watched for the mailman each day, and then, one afternoon, came idling up the laneway perusing the contents of a letter. Coming to the house, she slipped the letter into her apron pocket and no amount of persuasion could make her tell what was in it.

At supper-time she handed Father all the plates first, and urged him to take a little more of this and a little more of that. As he ladled a second nappieful of his favourite dessert, she gently said, "I had a letter from Mother to-day." We all looked up, filled with attention, but Father said, "Hmmm," and noisily strained another saucer of tea through his moustache.

There was a dead pause filled with the sound of the collie turning over on the front veranda and the clock changing gears as it came to the hour mark. Then Mother added, as casually as possible, "She wants us to come over to-morrow." Father droned, "Oh," and Mother, encouraged by this said, "Millie will be home to-morrow."

"Humph," came Father's reply, "I never could stand that husband of hers."

Mother, quick to seize any advantage, supplied quick as a flash, "He isn't home this time," and in a pensive sort of way, added, "I haven't seen Millie for over a year now."

Nothing more was said about it, but we heard voices after we went to bed and knew that Mother was persuading Father to go, against his deep-rooted hatred of having to get dressed up. When she came up to tuck us in, she said, "Better get a good sleep because your father is taking us over to Grandmother's to-morrow." We usually lay awake half the night thinking about it, but always managed to be up at four thirty the next morning as Father started out to do the chores.

Everything seemed to go wrong. That was the morning the brindle cow kicked the milk stool away from the head of the household. The cat seemed to pick that night for upsetting a pan of milk in the milk-house. The calves seemed to break out and get in the garden, and our belligerent Berkshire spent the night uprooting the chicken pens in the orchard and chasing the chickens half to death.

When the time came to squeeze into a stiff collar, Father was red-faced and belligerent. We generally managed to keep out of his way. His parting shot, as he went to hitch the team of drivers up, was, "Why don't your people come over here some time?" But Mother calmly went on packing a few jars of special preserves, and Father kicked the lane fence-post just to emphasize his words.

When it seemed that nothing else could happen, and we were travelling down the road about a mile from our front gate, with Father beginning to relax and notice the condition of the fields, one of us looked back. There was the brown mare's colt, loping along in a happy-go-lucky sort of way.

What happened then is better not told. Suffice it to say that after the colt was put in the stable, it took five miles of Mother's art of making conversation to make Father relax his face and quit complaining about the trip.

All things change, even in the country. The biggest change came with the advent of the Model T. Many words have been spilled in praise of the Model T. Some are earned and others are just plain sentimental. The years have glossed over some of the cantankerous qualities of the tinny monster. It's strange, that after a very few years, a person can even forget the "kick" of the crank that sent him spinning when the "Lizzy" was feeling on the temperamental side.

There was one time, however, when no car could compare with the Model T. That was during the spring season when our roads froze over at night and melted to a gooey morass during the day. I've seen a man get stuck with a horse and buggy, but my father was always able to get around in the "puddle jumper."

How thrilling it was when that brass-nosed car arrived at the house! There was a "sassy" quality about the flowing F on the radiator beginning the word Ford. The brass shone. The body was jet black and the side curtains with their mica windows were piled neatly on the back seat. The headlamps burned carbon with gas that came in some mysterious fashion from water and a chemical compound.

Albert Gibson, the cream-separator man turned car-dealer, brought the car into our front yard on a Saturday morning. Mother came out wiping her hands on her apron and even Grandfather, who had a prejudice against anything that challenged horses, ventured off the back veranda. Father, trying to appear casual, but really brimming over with excitement, made the announcement.

"Take a good look, folks. It's ours!"

With the selfishness of a small boy I immediately thought of how, for a change, we could scare *other* people's horses on the way to church or the village. Albert tried to coax Mother to get into the car. She refused and made a retreat to the house. The car salesman looked defeated but Father grinned.

"Don't worry. She'll be back."

Then he leaned over and whispered, "She wants to change her clothes."

A ride in a jet couldn't have compared with that first ride in the car. Mother, Grandfather and I were in the back seat, while Father rode up front with Albert. We scooted out and wheeled onto the road, fairly sailing down the hill. We coasted across the creek bridge and built up a fair speed for the grade.

"See the way she takes the hill?"

Mother was hanging on to the back of the front seat with one hand, clutching her hat with the other and looking frightened.

"We're going awfully fast, aren't we?"

Albert was elated.

' Oh no, ma'am. There's no danger. No blow-outs on this job."

There couldn't be blow-outs; we had solid rubber tires. At that time I didn't notice the bumps.

Father spent the afternoon with Albert in the big pasture field. The stock spent the afternoon in the swale, alarmed and confused by the whole thing. The cows gave a good deal less milk that night. Grandfather said it was because of the gasoline fumes. Mother said they were nervous.

She insisted that we take the horse and buggy to church the next day. My father was angry when his brother, who had been driving a car for a year, asked him if he had tied ours up before coming to church. That afternoon when Grandfather and Mother were having their usual Sunday rest, Father took off in the car. He made the roadway and got past the creek bridge but it stalled on the far grade and he ended up in the ditch.

Father was not a man to admit defeat. He mastered the driving and even learned the art of cranking, in spite of having almost put his shoulder out of joint when the spark was down too far. There was one thing he wouldn't admit. Those hard rubber tires gave one a bone-shaking ride. Mother began to pack the eggs for selling in oats in baskets so they wouldn't break on the way to the village.

There was something daring and graceful about the way that car could be steered to avoid the pot-holes and the places where the frost had pushed out corduroy in some of the roads through the long swamp. Grandfather said it reminded him of the way the daddy-long-legs navigated the creek water.

The novelty of it passed and the car that had at first been kept so neat began to be used to haul chop. Mother always carried a blanket to sit on. The mica was cracked in the side curtains. The fasteners were loose and on a rainy day the curtains blew like mourners' veils in a high wind. The paint was scratched and the brass nose of the radiator was dented.

Father bought later models of cars, so that the old one became a utility vehicle. It hauled chop and small pigs and calves. It was driven back to the fields with refreshments for the men. All year round it stood outside in wind, rain, hail and snow.

Nevertheless, when the later, faster models sat out the spring break-up in the driving-shed, that old brass-nose "puddle jumper" had a few weeks of glory. It fairly snorted with anticipation, dancing and skittering over the washboarded roads. It gave Father a great feeling of pride to sail past neighbours spinning in muddy laneways or stop and offer to do their errands in town.

The roads improved and modern progress doomed the old car. A pickup truck replaced it. I think that Father felt almost as sad to see the old car leave as he had when the last driving horse was sold to an itinerant dealer. There were no questions about the fate of either the horse or the car. No one had the heart to ask.

We can all overcome our emotion about the bygone steam whistle, but it is hard for us to forget the local train itself. That was an institution in our community. Starting thirty miles down the line, it chuffed and snorted along to the village station about seven thirty in the morning, and after leisurely taking on a mixed load, including people of all sizes, shapes and descriptions, it poked along to the city, arriving at mid-morning. About mid-afternoon it started back.

The local was called everything from "Gossip Special" to "The Toonerville Trolley." It was one of the few real conveniences we had in our part of the country. It was a mixed train with freight cars, passenger coaches, and express and mail vans. It was never on time, but strangely enough it was never really late, either.

The coaches had wicker seats that had been varnished often. I always left the train with a basket-work design in a vulnerable spot. There was a stuffy smoking compartment that smelled of cheap cigars and strong tobacco.

Ed Patterson was conductor on that train for over thirty years. He knew everybody that travelled on it, from the high school students to the babies that went to the city in their mothers' arms.

Leaving the station Ed always took a sharp look up the road in the direction of the village to make certain there were no stragglers. I have often seen him stroll up to speak to Jim Blake, the engineer, holding his watch in his hand while somebody came running down the road.

One never knew where that train was going to stop. People appeared at crossings with baskets of eggs or crocks of butter on their way to the city market, and the train stopped for them, before ambling along to the next station.

I can remember one day when the train sped along I asked Ed what the hurry was all about. He grinned and said that Jim was trying to get a little ahead so he could stop and try his hand for a big trout that he had spotted under the bridge over the river outside one of the small towns.

For twelve years that train never failed to blow its whistle at a place not marked in the railroad manuals, and for twelve years on the day before Christmas, Ed Patterson, Jim Blake and the brakeman stopped the train and went in to see Willy Jenkins, the crippled son of the section foreman. Not a soul complained.

The advent of trucks and cars doomed the local. School buses picked up high school students and so the line was closed.

A delegation of local big-wigs went down to Toronto to see a vice-president of the railway. He listened to them all and then asked, "How did you gentlemen come down to the city?" They admitted they had come in cars. That was the end of all hopes of getting our local back again.

27

OLD-FASHIONED EATING

WE SPENT A LOT OF TIME IN THE COUNTRY THINKing about food. We spent a good deal of time eating. Two of the highlights for me in connection with food was Sunday dinner and pickling-time.

There was something special about a Sunday dinner on the farm, especially when the whole family was invited to have dinner with Aunt Mary and Uncle Jim, a special event that occurred about twice a year. She was the one, as Father used to say, "who did things up brown."

The women-folk, with just a trace of jealousy, were quick to point out, however, that since Aunt Mary and Uncle Jim were childless it was a good deal easier for her to arrange a big dinner.

As a boy I was not interested in any other aspect of the

dinner than that it was a genuine feast. Even Mother, sitting in the rocker on the back stoop in her best dress, was inclined to agree that it was nice to go out and eat for a change.

Playing with the collie, I had that rib-busting feeling of anticipation, wishing that Father would make a move to get the Model T out of the driving-shed. As the minutes trickled by, it seemed that he would never go. Finally Grandfather broke the tension by saying: "Are we going to sit here all day?"

That did it.

Aunt Mary's and Uncle Jim's was one of those low, comfortable houses that look as if they had grown under the spreading elm trees. The front windows were like friendly eyes in the glassed-in veranda packed with flowers, and the front lawn, dotted with white-painted binder wheels circling great splotches of nasturtiums and petunias, spread down to the lane.

There were a couple of buggies in the barnyard. In prominent display was the Gray Dort bought by Uncle Tom as befitting the station of a man who, in addition to farming, made a fair amount of money out of insurance. The women vanished into the house, and as I went around to the shady side of the kitchen where the men clustered, there was a tantalizing smell of food.

After the weather had been disposed of as a topic, Uncle Jim lifted the door covering the cellar steps and disappeared. He reappeared with a gallon jug of a purple liquid called "cordial" in the presence of children, but which we knew to be elderberry "juice." In the cool shade it was pleasant to listen to the drowsy hum of voices.

Finally Aunt Mary appeared at the back door. She was a big woman with white hair and a pink and white face. Over her good dress she wore a freshly starched apron. After a ceremonial series of handshakes with the men and a few squeezes for the children she would invite everybody in for a "bite."

Extra leaves had been placed in the table, which had been set up in the front room. It was cool and a trifle dark in there, and it took a little time for our eyes to adjust so we could see the table. Autumn flowers bloomed in two vases dominating the array of dishes and cutlery on the white table cloth. Water glasses were beaded with sweat from the cold spring water.

Colour was supplied by plates of fresh, sliced tomatoes and small dishes of pickles ranging from tiny gherkins to healthy bowls of relish. Landmarks on the table were plates of freshly sliced bread standing beside the neat mounds of home-made butter ridged and scored with loving care.

Soup was something that made up a full meal at home, but Aunt Mary always served soup at the beginning of Sunday dinner. Fresh tomatoes had been simmered the night before and the finished product subtly blended with milk and cream. As I sat down before the steaming bowl, Aunt Mary deftly slipped a pat of butter to float serenely on the glorious pink and white surface. Grandfather, a noisy soup-eater, soon put his spoon into the empty plate with a clatter and announced: "By golly, that soup was good. Mary, you sure can make good tomato soup."

Then the food started to appear.

Aided by two volunteers, Aunt Mary brought in two roast chickens. Chickens! They were more like turkeys. One was placed in front of Grandfather and the other in front of Uncle Jim, for carving. Grandfather picked up the platter, put it over his own plate and pretended to start eating, at which point there was a groan from the youngsters. Those chickens were a delight to look at. They were shaded from light golden on the breast where they had been covered with strips of salt pork, to a deep brown on the drumsticks. When the thread over the cavity was slit, there wafted up an aroma of onion and sage from the dressing. As I sat there, it was almost impossible to control the digestive juices in my mouth.

Gravy-boats contained brown gravy speckled with tasty pieces of liver and small, crusty bits scraped from the bottom of the roasting pan. Mashed turnips came in bowls. Slices of turnip fried in salt pork gravy came on flat platters. Bowls of green beans contrasted with yellow wax beans, and corn on the cob was stacked on great plates like poles waiting for a "wood buzzing." Fresh chili sauce, fragrant with mixed pickling spice, came along, as well as apple sauce made from new apples and chilled in a jar in the spring.

The whole thing was a tantalizing blend of aromas that pricked at my nostrils and quickened my taste senses.

At these dinners conversation started out briskly, perhaps under the influence of the "cordial," but it was soon apparent that one couldn't continue to talk and keep up with the food.

Mumbled thanks of people passing and re-passing plates of food was a substitute for conversation. The older folks helped themselves, while the younger folks were helped. When the plate came in front of me, I had an almost uncontrollable desire to attack it ravenously. A warning frown from Mother made me sit tense, waiting until Grandfather had helped himself.

Then, as if by signal, the plates of hot biscuits would appear. Still hot to the touch, each was split and given a dab of butter. Aunt Mary was a person who believed butter was essential to good cooking. Uncle Jim used to laugh and say that they never had cream to sell because Aunt Mary used it all up to make butter for her cooking.

Having consumed one plateful and sopped up the brown gravy left on the plate, I naturally felt satisfied but that second helping was too much of a temptation. Even the women would say in a half-apologetic tone, "Well, maybe a little more chicken."

By the time dessert was brought on, everybody protested that he was "stuffed" but somehow our appetites would come back. The big white pitchers of fresh milk and pots of steaming tea—a deep, ruby-brown—signalled the bringing in of the pies.

Apple pie with a flaky crust, the apples immersed in a caramel-like syrup, accompanied by cheese that nipped your tongue vied for attention with pumpkin pie covered with great gobs of whipped cream.

Of course, that was only part of the dessert. No self-respecting country man would think of finishing a Sunday dinner without a slab of chocolate or white cake and some preserves. The bowls of pears spiced with cloves, or peaches in a thick, sweet syrup travelled up and down the table to be ladled out into "nappies."

Finally the meal came to an end. The children fidgeted until they were excused. The men lit their pipes, lingering to heap praise on Aunt Mary until she blushed. Then they went out to sprawl on the grass under the whispering elms. The women stayed at the table to chat and to pick at tiny bits of crisp chicken skin and have an extra cup of tea.

After that meal, even the children were subdued enough to find a spot of shade under the democrat or the wagon and talk about the mysteries of the world outside the valley, which were beginning to intrigue them.

Grandfather had acknowledged rights to the old sofa on the back veranda for a sleep, oblivious even to the flies playing hide-and-seek in his moustache.

Slowly and contentedly the afternoon wore on until chores beckoned and we started for home. Aunt Mary sent home with us for a cold supper slices of a cold ham which we hadn't even noticed on the table at noon.

The children had bags of home-made candy, sweet and delicious, but not even the candy could tempt us because we were still under the filling, comfortable spell of a Sunday dinner with Aunt Mary and Uncle Jim.

We were what my grandmother used to call "pickle-eaters." That means there had to be pickles on the table for all meals. At local threshings the ladies waiting on tables always made certain that the pickles were within easy reach.

Grandmother had a firm and solid feeling about pickles. She worked from the time the first cucumbers appeared, to late fall, putting down pickles that would add zest to winter meals. She made crock pickles, seven-day pickles, mustard pickles, cinnamon pickles, chile sauce, green tomato pickles and Heaven only knows how many more kinds, ranging from pickled beans to pickled crab-apples.

It seems a pity that a poet hasn't commemorated pickles in a fitting way. Certainly the whole procedure of pickling the cucumbers and assembling the spices and the tangy vinegar for the strange ritual must hold enough inspiration for a poet.

AUTUMN

MONTAGUE
WORLD'S

28

HARVEST-TIME

THERE WERE TWO THINGS ABOUT THE OLD-fashioned harvest that always thrilled a boy in the country. First there was the threshing. If the harvest came early, I had my own and two or three other harvests I could attend. If it was late and happened during the school session, I could always find an excuse to stay home.

The second thrill was the harvest excursion. The railroads used to have big posters like the ones for the Canadian National Exhibition. These were lures that I studied eagerly, as if by doing so, I could make myself old enough to go along. In our community the younger men went West each fall. If the harvest at home was poor or money scarce, even some of the older, married men would make the trip to western Canada.

The returning harvesters were marked men. Everybody

wanted to hear their stories of adventure. That's where many a small country boy first learned of the great expanse of grain fields that stretched for miles without a fence. We heard about sleeping in bunkhouses and of using straw as fuel for threshing machines.

The passing of the steam engine was a sad blow to the enjoyment of the harvest season.

"The Simpsons are going to thresh their wheat in the field."

An announcement like that was electrifying to the youngsters of the community. The sight of the threshing procession down the road was a signal to try and hitch a ride with the tankman. He drove the team of horses on the big tank that hauled water for the engine.

Occasionally I might get a chance to ride on the engine. I would be perched up on the small emergency tank or else clinging to the side with the saw that was used to cut up the rails and poles that served as fuel.

The separator was wheeled into the grain field, where the engineer backed the engine around expertly to the proper distance.

There were teams with loads waiting and, as one pulled up by the table, the belt was slipped on, the engine "pam-pom-powed" with extra effort, and the separator jiggled and jaggled into action with a great rush of small belts and pulleys, as well as the clattering of sieves and canvas. The fire-box belched fire and with a toot of the whistle the threshing started.

Soon there was a rustling sound as the straw was propelled through the blower and the golden grain started slithering out of the spout into a waiting bag.

The tankman was always a good companion. Most times the engineer and separator man had work to do, but the tankman could usually find time for a chat. At first, he was busy with the portable saw that ran on a belt from a small pulley, cutting up the pile of old fence rails and poles. Then he filled the boiler and two small tanks which he put beside the engine, and set out for the creek, river or pond.

A tankman was often a sort of nomad. He drifted from job to job. Some tankmen were lumbermen in winter. Some had been sailors on the Great Lakes. Others had tried farming but had given it up. All were great talkers and small boys were appreciative listeners. After manning the pump and filling the tank they were not averse to a dip in the water, a smoke or a snooze under a tree, coming to the alert when they heard a warning three blasts on the whistle. This was to show that the water supply was getting low.

Most tankmen just liked being around threshing machines. So did a local farmer known as "Steamer Bill" Jones. He never had much luck. When he planted a lot of potatoes there was rot or else the price was poor. He plunged into corn and borer took over. When he tried pigs the price dropped.

Bill Jones, however, loved to go to threshings. He never missed them, and it didn't matter whether he was ever paid or the work returned.

One day a car struck him on the main street of the village. He was in bed for three months and after that walked with a limp. He was finally persuaded to sue for damages, and when it came to court, a sleepy magistrate awarded him only one hundred dollars. The Perkins boy, who had just graduated in law, took up the case, made an appeal and won four thousand for Bill.

I guess Bill didn't know what to do with the money because he went to a hotel in the county town and proceeded to celebrate. Some time during the evening the conversation turned to steam engines and Bill bought one from a fellow celebrant who was a machine agent.

To this day, the story of how Bill and six friends drove the engine home for fourteen miles is a lively one. Fuel for the engine came from roadside fences. Fuel for the passengers and Bill came in a jug. They woke everybody up for miles around. Bill arrived in his front laneway, with whistle blowing, at daybreak.

That trip accomplished a number of things. He was dubbed "Steamer Bill" Jones and the name stuck with him. His luck changed and he got to be fairly prosperous.

Strange as it seems, he would never talk about buying the engine, which was kept, polished to perfection under a tarpaulin, but never started and used. Some people thought it was a sinful waste, but "Steamer Bill" used to spend his Sunday afternoons smoking and contemplating his famous engine.

A harvest meal had something very special about it. Perhaps it was the great bustle and hustle of preparation that made it an occasion. There was also the matter of pride among farm housewives as to who could prepare the best meal.

It was a known fact that some men had no trouble in trading work for a harvest. Their women-folk set a good table. A usual comment might be, "I never mind going to that threshing. Always two or three kinds of pie." The farmers weren't speaking in terms of having a choice of pie. They invariably helped themselves to every kind served. That was the lure.

A special event usually held during harvest-time was the church garden party or lawn social. Although the ladies of the parish probably spent a thousand dollars on material and effort in order to net five or six hundred, a garden party had many advantages that couldn't be reckoned in terms of money. An air of real excitement pervaded the community from the time the corner fence posts sprouted the handbills until the actual evening of the affair. The party line went from morning until night, but instead of gossip, there were recipes to be exchanged and plans for dishes, tables and serving to be arranged.

Bill Anderson volunteered to roll the church grounds while Ed Zinger and Joe Black put up the lights. We borrowed tables from the United Church and they borrowed chairs from us when they had the strawberry festival. Everybody pitched in to set up the booths and tables.

The kitchens were full of activity. It meant tragedy for some, because a good many older inhabitants of the chicken runs found themselves, after good long simmerings, reduced to chicken salad.

The only time there was friction was during the meeting at which assignments for handling the booths and the other responsibilities such as ticket-taking were handed out. It required a diplomat to soothe the sensibilities of some of the older residents who were not particularly gifted in mathematics, but who, for some reason or other, seemed inclined towards the jobs where making change was a requisite.

Tickets were always sold on prizes. The local MP got hit for ten dollars, some of the merchants donated items that were not moving very fast from their shelves, and the Bidwell sisters contributed their annual quilt.

There wasn't much work done around the farm on the day of the garden party. The lady of the household usually commandeered all the help she could get to pack up the food, plates, flowers and other necessary items. Then she had to be driven ahead of time to the church grounds, in her best dress, with a clean apron handy. The bunting was up, the stoves were going in the church basement and a few men were sorting prizes in the booths.

Boys became men in emergencies. A boy got a chance to do the chores on an equal footing with the men on the evening of the garden party, when everyone hurried back to the grounds for the supper. The farmers looked strange in good clothes. White shirt collars were startling against necks scorched to a deep copper colour by wind and weather. They stood self-consciously, looking at the snowy white tablecloths, the vases of flowers, and the shimmering bowls of jelly which were considered to be more attractive than nutritious. Some of the old-timers shook their heads a bit dubiously at the thought of a fifty-cent admission charge, remembering the days when thirty-five cents covered all they could eat.

What a supper! Here was found a variety to delight the heart of a trencherman in the season when potatoes, cucumbers, radishes, lettuce, and a host of other vegetables were at their peak. Here one found the best pickles of the community, from nippy mustard beans to crock pickles that fairly snapped when they were bitten. Ham, lovingly cured by old recipes, along with a host of other meats, was served with fresh home-made bread and butter, to be followed by the greatest variety of desserts imaginable.

The night wore on. The comfortable stupor brought on by eating too much was enough to make us sit without fidgeting through the concert and the interminable drawing of winning tickets, which always seemed to be held by somebody's cousin in Detroit or Buffalo. They might have been the only ones who bought tickets. Meanwhile, the games of chance such as the wheel of fortune and the fish-pond rolled on It was pleasant to see people enjoying themselves at an entertainment of their own making.

As the garden party continued, even the smell of frying hamburgers and onions lost its appeal. The younger folks took over the dance floor and the insects practically blacked out the light bulbs. It was time to gather up the dishes, silverware, and family and head for home in sleepy contentment.

29

THE FEEL OF FALL

FALL HAD A DISTINCTIVE FEELING ABOUT IT. I woke one morning to find that the maples and beeches had taken on a touch of colour. There was a rime of frost whiskers around the edge of the horse trough and the pumpkins sat like blobs of orange paint among the withered vines.

Fall mornings were full of sound as well. A tractor backfired in the distance, a train groaned up a grade and somebody beat a spoon on a dishpan to call the men to breakfast. A truck rumbled along the road and stopped to pick up milk cans. The pigs grumbled while pullets foolhardy enough to roost in the orchard waited for warm mash to help restore circulation. Those were mornings of calves bawling, and marsh fog and a clammy feeling to the hook of the barnyard gate.

Those were days of fall enjoyment and yet they were also

the days of the pre-invasion. The plunderers of this invasion were our city cousins. It was a phenomenon of the fall for which we waited like peasants who momentarily expect the castle residents to ride out and plunder.

The blast from the horn as the sleek, shiny car came swooping around the front gatepost sent chickens flying in all directions and chilled our hearts. Al and Ethel and their two children never wrote in advance. They were too cagey for that. It would have given us the tip-off to vanish for a day.

They were real city people. Their car was new each year and more gaudy-looking than ever. It had twin horns and electrical gadgets for doing all the work. When it had braked to a stop their two children were off like rockets to stir up trouble. Al looked natty in his new fall outfit and Ethel preened in her mink.

The first approach, in the established style of the traders and the Indians, was to give some gifts to the victims. Mother ended up with a half pound of dime-store candy and Father got five cheap cigars in a cardboard package. Al himself smoked cigars in individual metal tubes.

Then the propaganda started as we heard how tough it was in the city. To hear them talk you would think they were on a bread-line. Prices of everything they bought were rising, and wages hadn't kept up with the increasing cost of city living. Of course, it was different in the country where produce was free.

There were sounds of murder and mayhem from the direction of the barn. The children had managed to let the pigs out. They scattered, with the smart ones guzzling milk in the milk-house and the others getting sick on a heap of potatoes waiting in the garden to be bagged. The sow was chomping the cull apples in the orchard, which Father wanted for cider. He wondered . . . oh . . . why. . . . Oh why, couldn't they have just let the boar out? It was only for a moment, however, because one of them fell down the hay chute in the barn, and had to be comforted.

The allusions at the dinner table were pointed. It seemed that we lived like kings with ham and beef and all the different vegetables. The children meanwhile ate everything in sight, and poor Al wished with all his heart that he had never left the farm for the city. Father dimly remembered Al's aversion to work when he was on the farm. It was the beautiful fresh cream that struck Ethel. Apparently it was very difficult to get good cream in the city. When it was possible it was expensive.

After lunch I was amazed by the reminiscences of Al. It appeared that he and Father had been bosom companions at school. All Father could remember was the time Al squealed on him to the teacher, and Father got a licking for hanging two shiners on him.

The children were out on another pillage. Father and Al sat on the back veranda and Al spoke longingly of the wonderful apples in the barrels. Meanwhile, in the kitchen, Ethel was working her charm, and after a half-hearted mention of doing the dishes, accompanied by a remark of how badly chapped her hands were, she broke down Mother's resistance. They went down to the cellar and Al, with the instincts of a bloodhound, heard them.

"Say, I sure would like to see your cellar. I just get lonesome for the smell of a country cellar."

There were rows of jars of preserves and pickles and Father and Mother had to give in. The tithes had to be paid. As if by magic, Al discovered that there were boxes and bags in the back of the car.

"How much for a bag of potatoes?"

Like a fool, Father mumbled something about not knowing what they were worth. First thing we knew, they had swept us along. The potatoes were hauled to the car. There was also the matter of apples; they usually took a bushel of them.

"Now, you must keep account of this stuff because I want to pay you," perspired Al as he hauled out cabbages, beets, carrots and strings of onions.

"Oh," trilled Ethel, who, regardless of her mink, was hauling a carton of preserves, "don't forget the eggs, Al."

Then, with a patronizing smile at my folks, she said, "It's so nice to get some really fresh eggs for a change. I am positive that those stores in the city put it over on us with storage eggs."

The children didn't do so badly either. They came up from the barn lugging pumpkins. They simply couldn't do without them for Hallowe'en. They also discovered the ginger kitten that was a favourite of all the barn cats. When Ethel said they mustn't take it, they put on a howling dervish act.

They got the kitten. Father wondered why they didn't

bring a trailer for the purebred bull calf. Before the children had finally left, they had opened the chicken-house door and let out all the cockerels. It took three nights of tramping through wet grass in the orchard to round them up.

Carrying loads of produce to Al's car exhausted everybody, so Mother piled the dinner dishes that Ethel hadn't helped with and made a cup of tea. This gave Ethel a chance to tell all about the new fall fashions and Al the opportunity to tell Father what was wrong with him as a farmer.

"The thing that is wrong with farmers nowadays is that they're not progressive enough," spouted the expert. "You have to mechanize. Now, I'll bet I could start up farming tomorrow with proper mechanization and, of course, with my knowledge of management, and start it paying in a year. Mind you, it would be a really efficient operation and I'd put in cost accounting. You see, farming is really big business and there's no place in it any more for the little fellow."

Having exhausted their victims spiritually and physically they decided to head for home. The car trunk was full. The children squeezed in with the plunder in the back seat. The motor was started and goodbyes begun when Al suddenly shouted, "My goodness, I haven't paid you for the potatoes."

By this time Father was too exhausted to say anything so he waved in a general admission of defeat.

"Well now, I tell you what," countered Al, "when you come down to the Royal Winter Fair be sure and call us. We might have a night out. Sorry we can't put you up but there just isn't room in the apartment. But you be sure and call us."

"By all means, call us," chirped up Ethel, "I can arrange a tea for you at the Art Gallery. They're looking for new subscribers anyhow."

The motor raced and we stepped back from a flood of dust and exhaust fumes. We could still hear those twin horns blowing triumphal blasts when they got to the river bridge.

To me, fall was soup weather. An evening came every autumn when I noticed Mother putting the neck piece and knuckle bones that Father had bought at the beef ring, into the old, black iron kettle on the stove. After adding a generous portion of water to the meat, she chopped up a big bowl of vegetables. The last thing that night, she dumped these into the kettle and set it about halfway back on the stove.

Next morning the kettle was shoved to the back lid of the stove. Fighting my way home from school against a wind with teeth in it, I looked forward in anticipation to the ambrosia contained in that kettle. Sure enough, when I stepped into the kitchen the place was full of the wonderful aroma of soup. Sage, thyme and other spices had been added and the old black kettle was singing along with a merry bubbling sound within it.

"Gee, Maw., I'm hungry."

"Now, I don't want you to spoil your supper. You can have a piece of bread and butter."

She was only teasing, however.

"Can't I have something else?"

She paused and said, "I suppose a small bowl of soup would help to warm you up."

I didn't have to answer. She was already reaching for the soup bowl. With a stir of the ladle she filled the bowl to brimming.

Man, what a taste!

This was something to take the chill from my blood. The rich broth was thick with carrots and dried peas and beans that had been tenderized. There were generous portions of potato and chunks of pure meat. There were other vegetables, too—portions of cabbage and turnip.

There were no second helpings after school. However, that rule didn't apply at supper-time. The more I ate then, the happier she was, because she was proud of her "beef soup." That pot stayed on the stove until Christmas-time. It never became empty because there was a variety of ingredients going into it all the time. It was magical. At night before going to bed, Father often filled a bowl and sat down at the kitchen table. He liked, as he said, to "sop a little bread in it."

The only reason the soup vanished at Christmas-time was that there simply wasn't enough room on the stove for it. After the New Year, however, Father asked at the beef ring for some more knuckle bones, shank or neck, and the whole ritual began again. A highlight of the procedure was that on the first night after the soup had been started, I had fresh bread and butter and marrow from the bones. It was juicy and even more delicious than the bull's-eye candies that came two for a cent at the general store.

30

PARTY LINES AND MATCHMAKERS

MY FIRST REALIZATION OF HOW IMPORTANT THE PARTY line telephone was in rural community affairs came the winter I stayed with Uncle Albert and Aunt Martha on their farm in West Wawanosh Township in Huron County. My uncle had an attack of "the rheumatics" and I had to help with the chores and attend school.

One evening when I came in from the stable with Uncle Albert there was something missing from the kitchen.

"What happened to the telephone?" demanded Uncle Albert.

Aunt Martha pretended to be very busy around the stove as she replied: "The lineman was here and I . . . oh . . . I had him move it into the front hall."

"It'll be kind of cold in there in the winter-time, won't it?"

he said, but I noticed a smile around the corners of his mouth.

"It was a plagued nuisance dingling away here in the kitchen all the time," replied Aunt Martha as she put the platter of meat on the table. "Supper's on. Come and eat, now. Did you wash your hands?"

The latter was purely a routine question because she had seen me at the washstand. It served to change the subject from telephones.

I was amused by the incident because the evening before, a cattle buyer had called on Uncle Albert. They had sat in the kitchen because it was winter-time, and since we had not been expecting company there was no fire in the heater in the front room. The telephone rang—three longs and two shorts. There was a family exchange of glances.

It was Thursday evening and time for Sally Benson's boy-friend to phone her from town. She was my teacher and was engaged to the hardware clerk in town. The roads had been blocked for a month, so he telephoned every Thursday and Sunday evenings. Everybody on the line listened. It was as good as the serial in the *Farmers' Advocate*. We would sit around quietly while Aunt Martha, with her hand over the mouthpiece and the receiver to her ear, listened, turning around every so often to toss back a choice tidbit of gossip like: "Old Tom Kennedy that used to work in Riddell's store, died to-day. . . . He says he misses her terribly. Humph! He wants her to come and visit in town over the weekend. The school trustees won't stand for that."

The Thursday evening that the cattle drover came we missed our weekly instalment of the party-line romance. After that, if we had company and there was an interesting ring on the telephone, Aunt Martha would sit still for a few moments and then get up and start looking around as if there was something she had misplaced. Then she would walk into the front room and tip-toe through the far door into the hallway to the telephone. She always had a sweater handy in the hallway for such emergencies. We could always tell when she had reached the telephone because there was one squeaky board she never seemed able to miss.

After living in a "party-line" house we got to know which rings were interesting and important. Two longs and one short was no good. Tom Dyment was a bachelor and he used his telephone strictly for business. Four longs was a good one because there were three teen-age girls at the Thomson place and they had boy-friends. Everybody listened for two long and two short rings. That was Jack MacVicar and he was insurance agent, justice of the peace, pound-keeper and secretary of the school board. We could hear about a fire or a theft or strayed cattle or who was going to escort the schoolteacher to the dance at the township hall.

Abbie Jenkins was a notorious listener. Her telephone was placed at a convenient spot on the wall so that she could sit down and concentrate on her listening. She also had a great clock, whose ticking sound was a dead giveaway.

Abbie would never admit listening on the telephone and would often remark that it was a terrible habit for people to listen in on party-line conversations. Uncle Albert tricked her one time by suddenly stopping his conversation to the pig-buyer and saying: "Abbie, your clock is wrong." Before she had time to collect her wits she said, "It is not. I set it this morning by the school bell." Abbie was horrified, but the community had a wonderful chuckle.

The strange part about a party line in the country was that everybody listened but very, very few ever admitted that they did so. On the other hand, if there were a hint of tragedy, somebody sick or a fire they all chimed in without any thought of preserving their declarations of "no listening." So it wasn't entirely a bad habit.

I can still remember the time that Mother was sick when I was a very small boy. After she had been confined to bed for four days, Father called the doctor. Within an hour, four of the neighbour women came along to help. They didn't mention how they knew about her illness and my father didn't comment. He was mighty glad to see them. So was I, after a four-day diet of hard fried eggs, burned toast and tinned beans.

Another permanent fixture of the rural community was the confirmed bachelor. When I was a boy our permanent bachelors were Ed Peabody and Pete McCoy.

Ninety per cent of the women in our district complained about the hardships of marriage. They kept the party line burning with their expressed unhappiness. When they weren't complaining about their lot in life, they were trying to set up a scheme to enmesh our two bachelors in matrimony. Almost any time you picked up a "using" line you would hear conversation something like this:

"It's a shame that Ed Peabody isn't married."

"That house of his is a sight. Do you know, I don't think he ever washes a dish."

"Pete McCoy would make such a good husband for some woman. He's such a gentle man."

The women went to meetings of the Women's Institute, heard a paper on the art of applying wall paper, or how to make a table out of a nail keg, and then, over tea and cookies, they impatiently got down to the subject of real interest. Why didn't those two men get married?

Pete McCoy ignored them and went on his own way, happy by himself, and rather amused by the interest taken in him by the women. Some of the younger ones, addicted to soap operas on the radio, endowed Pete with a romantic tradition. They maintained that he had been "terribly in love with a girl who died in the flu epidemic."

This made a wonderful story. The truth was that Pete had always been afraid of women and would light out for the next concession whenever an eligible girl came around the McCoy homestead.

"Girls are just barley awns," Pete used to say when he was at the awkward, adolescent stage. "They give me the itch and I can't talk when they're around. They make me choke."

The candidate considered by district women the likeliest possibility for marriage was Ed Peabody. Pete had lived on canned pork and beans, fried bacon and potatoes, and strong tea for so long that ordinary food sickened him. Ed, on the other hand, was a real trencherman. Six pieces of pie were his normal dessert at a fowl supper.

This was the cue for the district women. If he liked to eat that well he simply must have a wife.

You could count on it, that when a new teacher came to our district she boarded at Maggie Henderson's. Maggie, a large woman with a perpetually red face, waited for two weeks and then invited Ed to Sunday dinner.

Ed always accepted. His black suit that age had greened was brushed and his shoes had a dull lustre from a copious application of water and lampblack. A blue shirt was topped by a white celluloid collar rendered immaculate by Ah Sing in the village. A black and white tie hung in the vicinity of a gold stud. His cap was dusty but quite presentable.

"Well, I'm sure pleased that we've got a pretty teacher at last," he always announced with a twist of his cap and a shuffle of the lampblacked boots.

The young teacher blushed. Maggie Henderson beamed and George Henderson grunted, "How did that east patch of oats turn out?" or something similar.

Ed retired to the veranda with George. Maggie told the teacher that Ed owned his own land, had the best stock and implements in the district and was known for certain to have a large bank account. The dinner was always a delight. Maggie beamed on Ed as he passed his plate back for a third serving of chicken and stuffing. He apologized and grinned sheepishly.

"Hope you forgive an old bachelor who isn't used to having such good food, Maggie. It sure tastes good."

Maggie was almost delirious. She failed to recognize the fact that Ed had employed this same statement for years. When the meal was over, Ed, having restrained himself to a mere two pieces of pie, retired to smoke and chat with George. The women did the dishes. Later, they came out on the veranda and conversation flowed in a desultory sort of way.

"Like to go and see the Keebushkin Falls?"

Ed always threw this question out in a casual way. The new teacher looked helpless. Maggie nodded vigorously. The teacher answered affirmatively in a squeaky voice. Ed took her down to where the creek splashed over several rocks that had been left over after workmen had quarried for the Presbyterian Church. After a decent period of observation of this phenomenon, Ed drove her back to the Hendersons'.

During October and November, Ed had at least four meals at the Hendersons'. The teacher was confused, afraid to say anything to the Hendersons about the fact that she already had a fiancé, and never quite certain about Ed and his intentions. Ed, meanwhile, had a fine selection of meals. The whole affair petered out before Christmas. The teacher produced her fiancé and Ed waited for the family who had a female cousin coming from the city for the holiday season.

One year my mother had a letter from her cousin Mabel. Mabel wanted to come and spend the Yuletide holidays on the farm. Mother was very happy about this and after a consultation wrote to say that she would be most welcome.

Two days later she started worrying about Mabel.

"There should be somebody to take Mabel out while she's here."

We didn't say a word. After a pause Mother spoke again.

"She's coming on the Sunday before Christmas. I think I'll ask Ed Peabody over. A good meal will do him good anyhow, and he has a car."

We didn't say a word!

Mabel arrived and Ed came for Sunday dinner.

"Well, I can see that prettiness runs in the family," he said when he was introduced to Mabel, and gave a jerk of the head to the rest of us. Grandfather snorted.

We had a wonderful dinner and Ed addressed at least two questions to the squat, giggling cousin.

"How are things in the city?"

"Can't understand why anybody wants to live cooped up in a city."

Mother perked up when Ed made the latter remark, and I could see her figuring that Ed was on the matrimonial road. As a result, he was invited for Christmas dinner. He arrived with a box of candy which he contributed to the general spoils of the day, but he added a sheepish grin for the benefit of Mabel, as if he were too shy to give it to her outright.

Ed had five dinners at our house during the holiday period, and he took Mabel to hear the Swiss Bell-ringers at the Anglican Church one night. A month later she wrote from the city to enquire petulantly why Ed hadn't written to her. She wrote at Easter and didn't mention him.

In the meantime, Ed had been eating at the Tylers'. Joe Tyler's widowed sister from Halifax had come for a month and Mrs. Tyler had been having Ed to dinner on a regular basis. The Keebushkin Falls were locked in the icy grip of winter, and so Ed had taken the widow to the Fat Stock Show and to a movie in the village.

Once when I was in town I had to wait with Father for some tractor repairs. We had a new teacher that year. Joe Anderson and Ed Peabody were sitting and smoking when Joe looked at Ed and smiled.

"Hear you had the new teacher out to the Keebushkin Falls."

Ed smiled and shuffled his chop-splattered boots.

"Pretty, this time of year."

Joe persisted as he said, "The teacher is pretty, too."

Ed smiled and said, "Maggie Henderson sure cooks good meals."

And so listening in and matchmaking have been established in the country for a long, long time.

31

A HIRED MAN CALLED SAMMY

EVERYONE BROUGHT UP IN THE COUNTRY EXPERIENCES tragedy sooner or later. My first brush with it occurred one autumn when I was quite young. That is why I hate those days in the late fall when the sun shines brightly without any warmth and the trees make funny shadows. They remind me of Sammy, our hired man. I wonder if Mrs. Jason ever thinks of him. I know my dad often did. He would stand at the kitchen doorway and look down the road toward the creek bridge and I can still see the strange furrows in his forehead.

Sammy wandered into the barnyard one day when Dad was fixing the gas engine. My father was short in stature, and sometimes short in temper, especially when it came to dealing with anything of a mechanical nature.

Sammy walked over to where Dad was working, and stood

silently. A lot of people said Sammy wasn't quite right in his head, but he certainly knew a lot about gas engines.

"You'll never make it work that way," he said matter-of-factly.

My dad, who had scarcely noticed him, looked up in exasperation.

"And I suppose you can fix it!"

"I can try."

Sammy picked up the wrench and looked at the machine. Then he fiddled around with a few nuts and bolts, adjusted a few things, gave the fly wheel a spin and the engine coughed into life.

"Sammy, you're a genius!" exclaimed Father.

The big fellow just smiled.

"Lots of folks wouldn't agree with you on that point. Jim Patterson and me just had a fight, and he says I'm the biggest fool he knows."

My dad and Jim Patterson were neighbours but they had never been close friends. In fact, on one or two occasions they had argued heatedly, although they had never come to blows.

"What are you doing now, Sammy?"

"Well, I don't know. I slept in your 'stack last night."

"Why didn't you come up to the house?"

Sammy shuffled his feet.

"Oh, I kinda hated to bother you and the missus."

My dad kept asking him questions until he discovered that Jim Patterson had let Sammy go and the argument had started when Sammy asked for some money.

"You see, I wanted a little money to get a new pair of overalls and a pair of boots, and I thought as how, since we had harvest off, he could pay me something."

"Wouldn't he give you anything?" asked Dad.

"Not a cent. Said I wasn't worth it."

My dad exploded then with some words that are not printable. He turned to me and made a gesture towards the house.

"Take Sammy up to the house and tell your mother to give him something to eat. Sammy, I need somebody to help me finish up the harvest. I'll pay you wages."

That's how Sammy came to stay with us. His full name was Samuel Worthington Adams, and he had been orphaned when quite young. He had lived with an aunt until she died. After that he quit school and went to work for Jim Patterson. He was a strange, awkward man with a quiet, drawling voice.

Mother gave him the room over the kitchen and on Saturday night Father took him into McLennan's Store to buy him new overalls, boots, two shirts and some other stuff. Sammy like my father.

"Your dad is a mighty fine man," he said to me. "He treats me just the same as anybody else. Your ma is kind to me, too. Do you think they'd let me stay here?"

I didn't know then that Sammy would stay at our place for a long time. I think Father had a soft spot in his heart for him. He was a good worker, too. He fixed up the sewing machine for Ma, and every time the binder broke he repaired it. Ma was a little worried because of the way some people were talking, but Dad settled it.

"Sammy is all right. He's a good worker and he has a lot more sense than a lot of these people who try to make fun of him. He's one of God's creatures destined to live in that strange place which borders between out-and-out genius and something else."

I liked Sammy. When Father brought home a pup, it was Sammy who trained him. He had a way of making animals do exactly what he wanted. One day I took the short cut home from school through the swale and came up along the creek. I heard somebody talking on the other side of a clump of willow trees. I tiptoed up to where I could look in without being seen. There had been talk about gypsies in the district and I was a little scared. Sammy was sitting by himself. He wasn't exactly by himself either, because he had a couple of rabbits up in front of him and was feeding them something and talking to them.

"Come on, little fellas. Come on, now. Sammy won't hurt you. You're good rabbits, aren't you? That's good, and here is something for you to eat. Pretty rabbits . . . pretty rabbits."

The light was streaming down through a gap in the trees.

The rabbits had edged up and were eating from Sammy's hand. I saw a chipmunk sitting on his knee. I slipped away as quietly as I could. Something kept me from disturbing them.

One day Sammy brought to the house a chipmunk that

had a broken leg. At first, Mother wasn't very fussy about having an animal around but when Sammy showed her that it had a broken leg, she softened. The chipmunk became a great pet around the place.

On an afternoon in late fall Father got into a tussle with a bull. Sammy was hoeing the late potatoes when we heard Father yelling in the barnyard. We all ran towards the sound. The bull had him cornered and was ramming at him with its horns. His smock was torn and there was blood running from a wound on his shoulder.

I was too small to do anything and Mother began to cry. Sammy picked up a piece of scantling and jumped the fence. He went after the bull and for a while it was like one of those Wild West movies. The bull charged him and he dropped the scantling. Then, he grabbed the bull around the neck. Sammy was strong. He grabbed the ring in the bull's nose and led it to the pen. His clothes were torn and dirty and he had a gash on his face. The back of one hand was all bloody.

"Sammy," my dad said in a gasping sort of way when he got his breath back. "You got a home here with us as long as you want. You saved my life."

Sammy thanked him quietly and went over to wash up in the watering trough. Ma made him come up to the house to put some iodine on the cuts.

A caretaker was needed for the school that winter. There wasn't much work at home, so Dad got Sammy to apply for the job. Shortly after, we heard that Jim Patterson had applied for his son Tom who was taking his first year of continuation at the school. Sammy and Tom Patterson put in for the same pay. It was all to be fixed at the school-board meeting.

My dad went to the meeting to put in a word for Sammy. I don't know all that went on at the meeting but from what I found out, there was quite a flare-up between Jim Patterson and my dad. Patterson tried to make out that Sammy wasn't fit to do the job. Father said that Patterson had used him for years without paying him anything. There was very nearly a fight. Finally, the school board gave the job to Sammy on the condition that Father be responsible if anything happened.

About the first of December, Mrs. Jason moved into the vacant house on the Leslie lot next to the schoolyard. There was a lot of talk about her coming back to live there. It seemed, as far as I could make it out, that she had worked for a man in the village who had a lot of money and had run away with him. He died in England and she came back.

"That woman was born to trouble," my mother said with her lips held tight, "There's some women like that in this life."

My dad didn't say anything. Sammy kept on with the birdhouse he was making for me to show at the winter fair in the county town. I was looking forward to seeing what this Mrs. Jason looked like. When I saw her I was surprised to see that she was very pretty.

One day when Dad was in the village with some grist for the mill, Mrs. Jason asked him if Sammy would shovel the snow for her and look after the fires in the house.

Mother was provoked when she found out that Dad had told Sammy about Mrs. Jason's request.

"Look," he said, "Mrs. Jason needs somebody and she's willing to pay Sammy good wages. There can't be trouble over that."

Sammy used to get up and put the fire on in the kitchen stove at home, go and start the fire in the schoolhouse and then go over to Mrs. Jason's to shovel the snow and look after the fires at her place. Tom Patterson used to tease him at school but Sammy appeared not to pay any attention to him.

"Understand that Mrs. Jason is pretty fond of you. You must have a real time with her, Sammy. When you going to get married, Sammy?"

I told Father about Tom's badgering Sammy all the time. He grunted and said, "Don't you say anything. That Patterson boy is a trouble-maker."

Mother was worried. She spoke to my dad several times about the way folks were talking about the Jason woman. She noticed too that Sammy was spending more time with the widow. Now and again he would be there all morning and when he came back for lunch there was always an excuse of some kind. He had had to fix a door or something.

"I don't think any harm can come of it. Sammy is brighter than most folks give him credit for. He'll be all right."

The winter moved along into spring. We buzzed wood on the Saturday before Easter. It was a pleasant day and at noon after the men had eaten they sat on the piles of wood, smoking and chatting. Jim Patterson was there that day. Sammy went down to water the horses and when he came back up, my dad was still in the house, eating at the second setting.

"I hear you're going to get married next week," Patterson said to Sammy. "You're a pretty lucky fellow to have such a good-looking woman go soft on you that way. She tells me that you're the man in her life."

Sammy's face reddened deeply and he started to scuff with his shoes at the sawdust.

"Yes, Jim, I certainly am a lucky man."

"Understand you're getting married next week. Can't hide a thing like that, Sammy."

My dad was standing on the back kitchen stoop with his hat in his hand. He looked angry. Then he put his hat on and walked toward Peter Farrier, who had the buzzing outfit.

I heard one of the men saying that Ab Henderson, the implement dealer, had been laughing about Sammy. I didn't understand everything that he said, but it seemed as if Henderson was friendly with Mrs. Jason, and she had been talking to Sammy about getting married. I was going to tell my dad, but I didn't know how to say it because there were a lot of things he would be mad about, if I said them.

The next Saturday, during the Easter holidays, Sammy came downstairs dressed in his best suit of clothes. My mother looked frightened and Father asked,

"Goin' into town, Sammy?"

Sammy turned red in the face again.

"I'm getting married to-day. Have to be there at eight this morning."

Father sent me outside. I waited around the corner of the back kitchen and after a while Sammy came out and walked down the road toward the creek and Mrs. Jason's house. After a while I went into the house. My mother was working and my dad was sitting in the rocking chair. He was just sitting there, not saying a word. I went outside to water the hens and gather the eggs. When I came back Dad was still sitting there. I looked at the comics in the newspaper.

About a quarter to ten Mother said, "Why didn't you stop him?"

Father said, "Can I tell him that somebody is dishonest enough to trade on his honesty? Should I tell him that he's not fit to marry Mrs. Jason, when he's worth more than twenty of her kind?"

The telephone rang. He jumped and picked the receiver off the hook. His face was set when he said, "I'll be there."

He took his hat and walked out the door. He stopped with his hand on the door knob.

"Mrs. Jason left town last night with Ab Henderson to get married. I thought there was something up."

He went out the laneway and started down the road. I saw a crowd around the creek bridge and ducked out of the back door. Mother called to me to come back but I went on anyway. I slipped around the barn and down the gulley and through the edge of the swale to the creek. I went slowly through the willows along the creek. I could see the crowd on the bridge without anybody's seeing me. Then I saw Sammy hanging by his neck from the crooked willow, all limp and crinkled up. My dad walked into the crowd and they silently made way for him. He took one look at Sammy and then he walked over to Jim Patterson and hit him. There was a dull thud when Patterson hit the planks of the bridge.

I was scared and ran through the willows and across the corner of the swale, back to the big stone pile in the far pasture. I sat down and cried until the tears wouldn't come any more.

32

CATS AND SPOOKS

CATS PROVIDE AMUSEMENT AND AMAZEMENT around the farm. They are, of course, a necessity No amount of modern invention seems to be able to keep rats and mice away from a farm. That's the task of our feline friends, who provide entertainment in the course of their duty.

A cat is the only breed of animal able to be a clown and yet keep its dignity. A cat can fawn on you, play stupid at the end of a string, and then, with a slight arch of the back and a disdainful grimace of that strange, whiskered face, walk away, leaving you with the distinct feeling that *you* have been playing the fool.

Around our place Tabby was the matriarch of the clan, and she accepted her role with full dictatorial aplomb. She was the only cat allowed in the house and she fought to keep that right against recurrent crops of kittens, most of which she had mothered. In fact, the only time she didn't appear in the kitchen was when she was busy producing another litter.

Tabby was smart. She slipped into the space between the woodbox and the back of the kitchen range and waited until supper and the work were over. Then, as the family settled down for the evening, she edged out to the mat in front of the stove. Stretching out to her full length, she composed herself for a quiet evening as a privileged member of the family. The tea-kettle burbling, the warmth radiating from the stove and the cat purring in contentment, added up to a perfect antidote for chilly fall weather.

Tabby was a show-off. She was never happier than when we discovered the presence of a mouse in the pantry. When she was summoned she stood up, arched her back and flexed her muscles like a swordsman, stalking with consummate poise into the pantry. Then she looked back at us, as much as to say, "Now, just run along and leave this to me." Crouching, freezing, sniffing and occasionally glancing back to see if the gallery was still interested, she worked around the pantry.

Next morning she was grinning as only a cat can grin. She toyed with her breakfast, just to let us know that the mouse mission had been accomplished.

One of Tabby's offspring was a fierce and independent spirit that we called Jesse James. His career as an outlaw began with a passion for climbing into the milk-house through a back window, where he invariably upset the cream pitcher. When this banditry was foiled he tried a new trick. Somehow or other he managed to get into the fruit cellar under the house. Jesse wasn't content to sleep on potato sacks or in a basket. He had to climb up on the hanging shelf where the preserves were neatly arranged in rows. In the middle of the night we heard a tremendous crash. I was convinced that the gypsies had gained access to the cellar. With heart pounding, I followed Father downstairs to investigate. On the cellar floor was a mass of broken glass and oozing fruit, the remains of four jars of wild strawberries. Jesse James was trying to hide behind the old butter churn. He managed to evade the broom handle and scooted through a broken window.

For at least two weeks we wondered where he had gone, but since he was only half grown, we imagined he had perished some place in the township. One day in the spring I saw him padding up the laneway from the river. By this time he was a full-grown cat, proudly bearing battle scars: a chewed-up ear, a gash around one eye which gave him a piratical appearance and deep scratch marks in the fur. Our Jesse had been out on the "hoot owl trail."

The family was of the opinion that Jesse had reformed. Within three days we heard an old hen in the orchard putting up a racket. Investigation found Jesse killing baby chickens, obviously to torment the hen. This time there was no alternative: Father aimed the shotgun but missed.

Jesse James was the persistent type. One morning while doing the chores I heard a terrific racket on the barn floor. Tabby, assisted by Mouser the Second and a brood of half-grown kittens, was disciplining Jesse. He was bleeding but game, and vanished when I came in sight.

Tabby gradually aged. She seemed to prefer holing up in the kitchen or the back woodshed to going out. The rats and mice were coming back to the granary. I tried coaxing Tabby to go out there and hunt them down. She wasn't interested. Once I locked her inside and discovered that she simply dozed on the grain sacks.

Then one day Jesse James appeared again. He was more battered than ever, but I noticed that he and Tabby strolled peacefully down the laneway to the barn. Later on Tabby came back to the house. It appeared that she had willed him the granary domain, because when I went to the barn, he was stalking a mouse. I withdrew.

Tabby passed away, comfortably curled up on the seat of the old cutter in the driving-shed. Minnie, a pretty young creature, inherited the kitchen domain because of her social graces.

Everything worked out well after that with Jesse James controlling the mouse and rat population in the granary and Minnie taking care of any mice that ventured into the house.

I have always thought that the days leading up to Thanksgiving were in many ways better than the day itself.

By that time we had got over the initial shock of school again. The determination of the teacher to make angels out of all her pupils soon weakened. She settled down and took a breather, knowing that Christmas concert-time was coming and would require a great deal of extra energy.

Horse chestnuts were in season and every desk drawer and pocket bulged with them. Some instinct made us hoard these items which were useless, except to the daring ones who carefully pared them out, inserted a hollow willow wand and then proceeded to smoke.

In spring there was always a good deal of work from cleaning grain to cleaning a winter-neglected stable, but in the two weeks before Thanksgiving, even Father relaxed. Harvest was over, the root crops would be pulled later and the silo filled. In the meantime he could enjoy, as somebody once said, "the sweet wine of autumn."

The slowing down of work was a signal for pleasant dawdling on the way home from school. Every day I saved a ripe tomato and a twist of salt in newspaper from my lunch and spent a long time at the culvert watching the lazy chub and minnows slipping through the greenish-dark water.

Then I picked up a stick to swish at the ripe goldenrod with, and sent the mullin seeds flying as I walked through the swamp section of the concession to come out by the slaughterhouse.

If the butcher wasn't killing a steer for the beef ring on that day, I could investigate for the umpteenth time the old, deserted log house. Mustiness, spider webs in profusion and mice to be chased and old catalogues with strange pictures of men with wax moustaches and women wearing tightly drawn corsets were the main attractions.

There were plenty of apples at home but I had to make a raid on the Jenkins orchard, take a couple of wormy ones that lay on the grass and then make a run for it as old man Jenkins came hobbling towards me with his ancient hound coughing beside him. It was fair game and both sides knew it.

I cut through the fields and tried to sneak up on the groundhogs that were storing up their winter fat. They lay by their burrows on the sunny side of the Big Hill. Then I raced to the back kitchen. There was a warning cry from inside and I paused. I had to pause; my nostrils were catching the wonderful aroma of pickles and the deep and penetrating scent of dark, winey grapes simmering in the hot cauldron on the kitchen stove.

Mother appeared with a big spoon in her hand, her face red and perspiring. Brushing back the stray wisps of hair over her forehead, she said, "What kept you so late?" This called for a shuffle of feet, because in those wonderful, pre-Thanksgiving days after a bountiful harvest, no explanation was required.

"I suppose you're hungry?"

Forgotten were the tomato and stolen apples.

"Well, I don't want to spoil your supper but I guess some bread and butter wouldn't hurt you. Now, go along down and get some milk from the milk-house. I need some for supper."

At this time of the year the milk-house was a sheer delight. Early ripened pumpkins vied with apples in barrels. Overhead on the suspended shelf were pickles and preserves of every kind. There was also a very large crock of what were called crock pickles which I was warned not to eat before they were cured. Mother said they might be poison, but they always tasted better, or seemed to, in a poisonous state.

Suddenly I remembered the house and the fresh bread. I rushed to take the thick, larrupy cream from the top of the milk in the flat pan and fill a pitcher full of milk. For some miraculous reason, I raced to the house without spilling it. Through the back kitchen with its heavy incense of pickles and preserves, and into the kitchen I ran. There were thick slabs of bread still warm from the oven with butter melting on top. In a convenient place was the extra half-jar of chile sauce left over from the preserving. Who could resist a dab of this tantalizing mistress of all kitchen preserving, its tomatoes delicately laced with all kinds of spices?

There were other things, as well, in those days before Thanksgiving. At an early Thanksgiving the stock were still not stabled and when I went into the stable, it had an air of mystery about it. There was a dry smell with heavy overtones of the lingering fragrance of manure. The old bull rattled his chains and the calves in the far stalls bawled loudly to exercise their lungs.

Upstairs the mows were packed with straw and hay. The sunlight coming through innumerable knot-holes in the siding sent down dust-laden beams. There was adventure here in the mows, especially on the uppermost timbers where the cooing of the pigeons came with a fluttering sound. The granary was fat and full of grain and I plunged my bare feet through it to feel the tickle between my toes.

Those were the golden days of fall. The leaves had started

to turn, and I knew that we were on the threshold of the miracle of autumn and that peaceful time when a countryman realizes the good fortune of a good harvest.

The days approaching Hallowe'en were always days of deep delight. There were not many occasions in the country when a small boy could get out at night. There really wasn't any place to go. Besides, it was usually pitch dark, and while the older boys could walk around with a show of bravado, it wasn't easy for a young lad.

Hallowe'en was different. There were always some older youngsters willing to let me tag along. It was a ruse on their part because they managed to slip away after I had been dropped at home, to have some "real fun," such as dismantling the Hendersons' wagon and putting it back together again on the roof top of their driving-shed. There was also the privy belonging to the Malloy sisters that had to be upset. This was traditional sport.

Getting ready for the nocturnal trip was a major part of the fun. With an old pair of Father's trousers, a swallow-tailed coat found in the attic and a battered old derby hat, I completed the disguise with part of a cut-down black lisle stocking belonging to Mother. Small holes were cut for my eyes, nose and mouth. I was certain no one would recognize me when I held out my basket for the spoils.

It was getting dark out and I waited anxiously for my cousin Mary or Bert to come along to take me in tow. As the hands of the clock turned, I was afraid that perhaps my parents wouldn't allow me to go out at all. Then there were eerie whoops and a mysterious face appeared at the kitchen window. The shivers danced jigs up and down my spine.

It was black outside. I could see the other youngsters crowding around as Mother handed out little packages of cookies and home-made fudge. First thing I knew, I was trudging down the road with the other kids, all of them mysteriously garbed. It was dark, but a moon was riding up from behind the old elm trees, playing hide-and-seek behind the black clouds that looked like witches flying high in the sky.

Near the swamp the youngsters bunched together in a kind of mutual protection pact. After all, we were pretty young and there were plenty of spots in the dark and mysterious woods where we could be ambushed. Every inky shadow behind the stark reeds could be a gang of older boys. We walked on, relieved by the sight of the end of the swamp. Then, just as we appeared safe, howling dervishes came jumping up from the sides of the road, swirling around us in dark waves. I knew it was just the older boys but my heart bobbed into my mouth. Anyway, the sound would have done credit to an Indian ambush of a western wagon train.

After a time it grew quieter, and it was noticed that some of the younger ones were crying. The sound of small children bawling seems to have a soothing effect on big boys bent on mischief. The band had increased now and I noticed that the older boys were pairing off with the girls.

The home of the minister was our first call. It was always good for some packages of "boughten" candy. The Cameron laneway was too long and besides, old Mr. Cameron lived alone. On the other hand, everybody had to go and call on the Burts. They were crusty, and Mr. Burt had been known to fire a shotgun into the air in an attempt to frighten marauders.

We crept silently up the laneway. Somebody tripped and fell on the frozen road. Somebody else whimpered. The air was pregnant with a great sense of adventure. Then a dog started to bark and half the brave band made a race down the road. The kitchen door opened and the old man stood peering into the dark.

The retreat was very disorderly and when we re-convened on the roadway the older boys were quick to say, "Ah, they wouldn't give you anything anyway."

Trudging in and out of laneways was a real job. I was sweating under the weight of my clothes and the black stocking was itching my face. The basket was getting heavy with cookies and candies and apples but I dared not give in and admit that I was tired. So down the road I went. Soon I saw the village ahead.

By now our interest in night life was waning. There was an attempt to slap some soap on the general store and then I realized that I was really tired. I also realized that the older boys and girls would be just as glad if I were to go away and free them of responsibility for me.

Then I spotted Father. Just by chance, mind you, sheer chance, he had come into town. The horse and buggy standing by the hitching rack in front of the Commercial Hotel was a welcome sight. Then I noticed that other parents were also in town.

By the time the horse had come to the grade at the edge of town I was sound asleep. When I got home I was taken into maternal custody and stripped of disguise. A glass of warm milk was a welcome relief after the variety of weird materials in my basket.

Bed was a wonderful haven and I went to sleep dreaming of witches and dragons. But I also knew that for several days I would linger in that wonderful world of imagination.

It was never hard to convince myself that I actually helped to put the light wagon up on the driving-shed. I could even convince myself that we must really have scared Mr. Burt. As for the outdoor conveniences of the Malloy sisters, how could anybody doubt that I was kingpin in the whole operation?

Yes, the dark, mysterious doings on the night when witches flew on brooms and goblins played mischief with mere mortals were always remembered with a certain amount of poetic fancy.

33

MEMORIES

EVERYTHING MUST COME TO AN END. IT'S impossible, however, to finish off a reminiscence by simply saying "The End." There are two recollections which have remained so firmly in my memory that I think they deserve a place in this final chapter.

There can be no experience in life to match the first time a boy is allowed to take a trip by himself. Like the fledgling from the nest who has always accompanied his parents, he is thrust out to make do on his own. It can be a happy experience or a sad one. It will be memorable.

On the day of the county fair, the year I was fourteen, I awoke when it was still dark and although I didn't have a clock, I knew that it was time to get up. This was a day that I had to enjoy to the full. Dressing in the dark so as not to wake my father and mother, I seemed to be making a tremendous amount of noise.

"Now you must get a good breakfast," urged my mother.

"Can't see why you wouldn't go with your uncle," grumbled Father. "He wouldn't have minded a bit."

I knew my uncle wouldn't have minded, but I did.

This was to be my trip and I was going to walk the twelve miles to the county town. In the weeks before the occasion, I knew I had to make the trip. I think my father understood. At least, when I managed to escape on the day of the fair, with the parcel of food prepared by Mother, he came out on the back stoop.

"Be a good boy," he muttered, and then pressed something into my hand which later turned out to be a dollar and a half in silver done up in a twist of newspaper.

Wondering at the strange ways of parents, I struck off down the road. It was still, with pre-dawn stillness, and the air had a nip in it. My boots clattered on the gravel, causing the Websters' dog to set up an unholy row as I walked by. His barking gave rise to the story that a tramp had passed that way.

In the strange way of autumn, the sun peeked up over the rim of the hills, quickly warming the air. The country-side began to come to life with thin plumes of smoke appearing from farm kitchen chimneys. The early freight-train groaned and dogs barked at the sun like ancient ritual worshippers. When I came over the top of the Big Hill by the river, the thought of some cold spring water became enticing. Turning into the flats towards the spring I found a scene that I will never forget.

One of those old hump-backed Model T's, the first sedan style, was parked by the spring. A man on a camp stool sat beside a fire which had a kettle boiling over it. He was peeling onions and throwing them in the pot. On his head he wore a battered derby. His trousers were grey and he wore a red, swallow-tailed coat over a woollen undershirt. I was walking on, as if going by him, when I noticed a tent pitched on the river side of the car.

"Morning, son. A fine day if ever there be a fine day," he sang out and I caught a whiff of the cooking smell from the pot. Never in my entire life have I smelled anything as appetizing as the aroma from that kettle.

Just then the tent flaps came open and a girl stepped out. In bare feet and wearing pyjamas she stretched, exposing a strip of bare skin. While I stood and gaped she smiled at me, threw back a mop of yellow hair, grabbed a towel from the makeshift clothesline and ran for the river.

"My daughter, Tina," said the man. "Sit down, boy, and take a load off your feet."

His name was Fotheringham Montague and he was an herbalist. I listened, becoming aware from time to time that my mouth was hanging open, to the story of his life. It appeared that he was dedicated to the cause of humanity and that he would be appearing at the County Fair. Tina came back from the river wrapped in the towel, flashed me a smile that made my cheeks flame, and then vanished inside the tent.

The tent was packed after breakfast, the fire extinguished, the old Model T was loaded and we sailed off down the road.

From the time that Fotheringham Montague bluffed the three of us into the fair grounds without paying admission, until the event was over, the day was a mad whirl. There was a furious argument between the secretary of the fair board and Montague who, famous or not, was so broke he couldn't pay the small exhibitor fee. I put it up, and in the instant of handing over the money, felt like a silly, gullible fool.

I found myself dressed up in a cowboy outfit and introduced as the son of Montague. For the benefit of the public the story went that I had been a sickly child but after being liberally dosed with MONTAGUE'S MARVELOUS MEDICAL DISCOVERY I had blossomed out into a "fine, strong boy with the strength of a young bull."

It was all a haze and at the centre of the hypnosis was Tina, who danced, sang and squeezed my arm. I was hopelessly in love with Tina.

The medicine sold and sold. The stock ran out and Fotheringham Montague handed me ten dollars and gave Tina ten. Then he vanished, saying that he had to get ingredients for a new batch.

Tina just shrugged her shoulders and said, "He's gone to the hotel. Come on, kid, we might as well see the fair." That was a day of days. Tina knew everybody in the small carnival side-shows and we had "everything on the house." In addition, I was followed at a worshipping distance by a whole pack of schoolmates who stared at us in envious curiosity.

The day came to an end with a meal at the Chinese cafe. Then we waited in the little park for her father who seemed to be entertaining everybody in the bar of the Royal Hotel. I pleaded with her to be allowed to travel with them but she smiled a little sadly and said, "It's no good, kid. You get your education. This is no life for anybody. I wouldn't be here only Maw is dead and someone has to look after him."

She was only sixteen, two years older than I was myself, and yet she seemed old in a wise way, and when Fotheringham Montague came back to collapse into a snoring sleep in the back of the car, she gravely kissed me and then drove out of town. I walked home in the black night, a spot near my lips still burning from the kiss, knowing that there would be a full-scale investigation into my actions at home and yet not caring.

My last reminiscence spans boyhood and manhood. Although the farm was the focal point of my small boyhood, the village and the people who lived there slipped into my life partly because of Continuation School and partly because of my natural, youthful curiosity.

As a boy I saw the community's veterans when they came home after the First World War. They carried dunnage sacks and were dressed in khaki with thick, heavy greatcoats, puttees and heavy boots. Most of them had souvenirs of swords or plumed German helmets. The reeve of the village made a speech and the ladies of the various churches, forgetting denominational lines, put up a spread in the village hall. Each man was given a pocket watch, suitably engraved.

For a time we saw the men walking about with their uniforms on. Later, they wore their uniforms with the insignia pulled off. Gradually even those identifying marks were gone, and then the veterans melted back into the community, wearing the overalls and smocks customary in rural areas.

It was typical of Ozzie Pollock that he slipped back into the village without any fanfare. Someone at the grist mill said that the station agent had seen him getting off the train from Toronto. Somebody else had seen a light in his window, in the shack down past the sawmill. The hero of the village had come home unheralded.

Ozzie and Mrs. Pollock had lived in a house that everybody called "The Shack," that was situated just past the sawmill and not far from the railroad depot. Mrs. Pollock, as she was called out of courtesy, was Ozzie's mother. His father wasn't known in the village. Everybody liked Stella Pollock. She bore her burdens in quiet determination, making a living by doing housework and laundry. For a month each year she made up the rooms at the Commercial Hotel while the hotel-keeper's wife was on vacation.

Ozzie had been a small, quiet youngster with big eyes in a pale face, who always seemed to be wearing clothes that were too big for him. They were hand-me-downs from the banker's and grist-mill owner's families, given as extra rewards for Stella's dedicated work.

At first he had a rough time at school, but he was so passive that the tough kids tired of picking on him and he managed very well after that. He was only sixteen when war broke out, but he was one of the first in the village to volunteer. I heard that his mother pleaded with him to stay home. It seemed foolish to put such a weak little fellow into the army, but as she so often said in later days, "He may have been small but he certainly was determined."

People were inclined to nod and reserve their opinions of that statement but soon the stories started coming back from overseas. Little Ozzie had been in the thick of things. In 1915, when the dreaded word "gas" was first known, Ozzie was decorated for bravery at Ypres. Marshal Foch praised the Canadians, and people in the village who had never paid any attention to Ozzie started taking off their hats to his mother, whom they had previously tolerated as a sort of Mary Magdalene.

In 1916, when Lloyd George praised the Canadian troops after the Battle of the Somme, at least half the people in the village thought he was praising Little Ozzie because he had been decorated again. The fighting advanced to Vimy Ridge where he was mentioned in dispatches. Then after Passchendaele there was no word from him. Stella was working at the hotel at the time, and when people asked about Ozzie, she just shook her head with tears in her eyes.

Little Ozzie popped up again, however. A wire came for his mother saying that he had been wounded and was in hospital in satisfactory condition. This was just about the time that the senior Doctor Macdonald, going into the Commercial to have dinner one evening, noticed Stella, who was going home after her chambermaid duties. He commented on her cough and when she tried to evade him he stopped her. The old doctor was a formidable two hundred and eighty pounds with great whiskers. He ordered her to bed and then to hospital. It was too late because she was in an advanced stage of tuberculosis and had been hiding it from everyone, afraid of the cost of doctors and hospitals.

She died in the spring of 1918 about the time we heard that Ozzie had gone back into action as a sergeant. Matt, down at the newspaper office, was commissioned to write to the soldier about his mother, and as he said afterwards it was the hardest thing he ever had to do in his life. It took him all one night because he wanted to tell Ozzie of how a whole village felt and the guilt they inwardly bore for the years of ostracism they had meted out to Ozzie and his mother.

Then Ozzie came home. He kept to himself. When he came uptown for groceries or a newspaper he was polite, and as quiet as when he had been a pathetic small boy in clothes that were too big for him. The town council debated and then decided to break the ice by presenting him with a watch. I wasn't there but I can just imagine the fumblings and the fiddlings as the reeve and four councillors descended on "The Shack."

When they came back they simply reported that Ozzie had taken the watch and thanked them. They said the place was as neat as a pin and cosy. There were a lot of books and some war souvenirs and that was about all they could say. Ozzie firmly refused a testimonial dinner. He also refused to talk about the war.

There was a great rush to get a war memorial up for the second anniversary of Armistice Day. It was to show the figure of a Canadian soldier in battle uniform, standing on a base of granite, with the names of all who had served on one side and all who had died on the other. It was a fine monument and the only reason they got it on time was that the brother of the banker's wife owned a monument works in Toronto.

It was on that day that Little Ozzie appeared with his uniform and the medals dangling from his left breast pocket. They were mighty impressive. Even the Presbyterian minister, who had been a padre, had a hard time keeping his mind on the prayer after he saw Ozzie. The little man looked to be seven feet tall and stood out from the twenty-odd other veterans.

Next day he got a job in the sawmill and he worked there for many years. He never spoke of his war record and even when he was given a write-up in a national magazine he didn't comment. Yet, on each Armistice Day he appeared at the cenotaph with his medals in full array. People used to say he was a "queer one."

Life had given Ozzie a strange sensitivity. Maybe it was that same sensitivity that had made him a great soldier. I can remember one thing which makes me believe that he had great feeling for the war and all who served in it.

Coming through the village, late one November 11, I saw a figure standing in front of the memorial. It was difficult, in the cold November moonlight, to distinguish between the figure on the ground and the one above. Both were motionless, like grey ghosts in the moonlight, and by some strange trick of fancy I imagined for a moment that there was a long column of them stretching into infinity.

It was then that I knew Ozzie's secret. His real friends didn't live in our village.